Jump Start This Church!

How to Go from
Declining Church to Dynamic Church

*Reverend Jane A. Willan
and Peter G. Dennis*

Printed in the United States of America
ISBN: 978-1-935254-94-2

Authors' Photo by Mary Dennis Photography
        Location courtesy of the Grafton Country Store
Cover Design by Vorris Dee Justesen
Edited by Sammie Justesen
Book Design by Nadene Carter

First printing, 2014

Contents

Preface

The situation is dire.

With young families more likely to choose soccer over church on Sunday morning and more than five thousand churches closing every year, *church* as we have known it is fast disappearing. Pastors need new skills and tools to grow their churches.

In other words, pastors and church leaders must learn how to sell.

Few pastors would be proud to say they're in sales. Yet all pastors wish to *sell* their churches. In other words, all pastors long to nurture their churches into significant growth, creating larger, stronger, and more financially stable congregations. A solid sales approach is as necessary to the successful pastor as preaching and pastoral care; yet pastors do not learn the art of sales in seminary.

Jump Start This Church! to the rescue.

This book is about teaching today's pastors to *sell* their churches; it is about packing the pews, generating money for missions, and building a thriving community presence.

Peter and I bring divergent perspectives to this project: I approach it from the viewpoint of the parish minister, while

Peter approaches from the world of professional sales. Our objective is to fuse these perspectives into a playbook that shows how churches can grow and thrive in 2014 and beyond. The two of us don't always agree, but we hope our spirited, thought-provoking style will stimulate discussion for both church-goers and pastors and renew the faith in what the church can accomplish *if sold correctly.*

Today's churches face an urgent situation. But negative trends can be reversed—not through one more book written strictly from inside the walls of the church, but by the collaboration of the secular world of sales and the religious world of faith.

Jump Start This Church! will make it happen.

Reverend Jane Willan

~ ~ ~ ~

This book is dedicated to our spouses Don and Mary.
Without them, this book wouldn't have happened.

Chapter One
The Awful Church

By Jane

"No way would I come here," I said to my husband, stepping back from the dirt streaked window of the old church. "I'm taking it off my list." Don and I were vacationing in New England and had stopped in Grafton, Massachusetts. I wanted to take a look at the Congregational Church of Grafton—a top candidate on my list of churches that were seeking new pastors. I was just starting a job search. As a parish minister in The United Church of Christ, my hope was to find a church in New England. Don and I were spending a few days driving around the area, getting a feel for the communities in which each church on my list was located. We were excited about Grafton. The community and the church seemed a perfect fit for us.

With high hopes, we drove into Grafton and were delighted with the beautiful town green circled by picturesque New England buildings. But then I saw the church. After leaving our car in the church parking lot, I walked around the building. Paint peeled off almost every inch of its exterior walls. Cloudy windows showed a dark and cluttered fellowship hall, dead plants lined the window sill, and even the doors looked battered.

Church buildings neglected to such a degree meant only one thing: a dead and dying congregation without the resources—emotional or financial—to do anything about it. An exhausted building, an exhausted congregation.

"Let's go," I said, heading to the car. "I've seen all I need to."

"Are you sure?" Don asked. He stood on the sidewalk with his back to the church looking out across the town common. "This town green is beautiful."

"No," I said pulling the car door open. "I want a church people care about. Look at this place—it's a dump." And with that, we left behind the quaint and welcoming town with its dilapidated congregational church. Little did I know I would find my way back to that weary old building and embark on one of the most rewarding parish experiences of my career.

When Don and I left our home in Iowa for that New England vacation, I was carrying what felt like my own dark secret: we were heading to Massachusetts where he had an interview for a job he wanted and was likely to get. When we returned, I would be telling my church in Iowa I was leaving. The Iowa church had been an incredible parish: dedicated to growth, energized, and conflict free. I was employed by a dream church, and I knew it. I had been a parish pastor for ten years, and felt very comfortable in Iowa. And yet, as I said goodbye to the people of my church to leave for vacation, I knew in my heart I would soon be permanently leaving them. Don had moved for me twice. Now it was my turn to move for him. But leaving my congregation would be heart wrenching.

I took with me on our vacation/job interview, a list of churches that seemed to fit my desires as a pastor and my skill set. Don had organized the list into a spreadsheet with categories such as location, size, salary, and Open and Affirming status. As we spent two weeks in New England visiting friends and relaxing, we also stopped at almost every church on my list. I wanted to stand in front of each church and see how it felt. That's when I marked the Congregational Church of Grafton off my list. Don did a five-hour interview with a company outside of Boston and he felt it went well. And as we headed home, they called and offered him the job. How soon could he start? He was ecstatic. I was heartsick. Thus began the long and wretched process of telling my congregation I would soon be leaving. Any pastor knows that is a terribly painful moment in one's journey with a church.

In my denomination, pastors generally give ninety days' notice. As one of my friends in the corporate world said, "Three months is a long time to be a lame duck employee." It was three months filled with goodbyes, well wishes, and sometimes for me as I looked around my beloved church—shock. But as I said goodbye, I also sent out my profile to the churches left on my list. To my encouragement, the profile was well received. I had lots of positive responses and interviews, and by late September, an offer from an excellent church. But I turned it down. Something didn't feel right. At first it had seemed perfect—everything I wanted. And then I knew it wasn't. Although saying "no" was the right thing to do, it also meant I was back to square one.

Don had already moved to Massachusetts and started his new job, and I was at home in Iowa making arrangements to leave and join him. It was early October and we both thought I would have a church by then. I didn't. We re-evaluated the spreadsheet. Four months had passed since our drive around New England looking at churches. That trip seemed a distant memory, and my feelings of anticipation and hope were eclipsed by the painful experience of saying goodbye and leaving the community I loved. Worse, I had hit a wall with Search and Call. Should I stop the process? Take a break from it?

Then one evening on our nightly Skype call, Don said he was looking over last summer's spread sheet. He asked me why I didn't send my profile to Grafton. "Remember?" I said. "It was the awful church."

"No," he said. "That wasn't Grafton. Or was it? I think the awful church was that one further south."

We went back and forth and I suddenly couldn't remember for sure.

"I'm positive we've never been to Grafton. You're thinking of somewhere else. I'm going to drive there after work and check it out," Don said. I clicked off Skype and checked the webpage for UCC church profiles in the Massachusetts Conference. The Grafton church certainly did seem like everything I wanted: passionate, social justice oriented, not yet Open and Affirming, but wanting to be. Plus, it was the right size, had a parsonage, and followed conference guidelines. What could be better? Was I thinking of the wrong church? I must have been. Anyway, my options were narrowing. I would leave my church in Iowa in three weeks and I had nothing. The next afternoon, Don texted me that he was about to leave for the town of Grafton to "check it out" and while he was en route, I sent my profile to the Grafton church.

That evening some good friends took me out for a final farewell dinner and when we were on our second bottle of wine, Don texted me. "You would love this place, Don's excited message read. The other women were interested, and the texts began to fly back and forth. As we poured more wine, I read each one aloud.

"Cool coffee shop on the green."

"The common is like a postcard of New England."

"Lots of activity."

"Seriously, this is NOT the awful church."

"You're sure?" I needed to know. Could I have nearly missed a good opportunity because I mistook it for another church? We had looked at lots of churches the previous summer.

The next text was a picture of a beautiful white New England church bathed in the glow of a late sunset. "See? Too nice to be the awful church." Don had taken the picture from across the town common. And it was beautiful. Majestic even. A tall steeple outlined against the dark blue of the late evening sky.

"Okay. Great!" I texted back. I was relieved. So the church that had looked so neglected was a different church after all. This church had everything I wanted and its search committee was still reading profiles. I felt hopeful again. Several more pictures beeped onto my iPhone. It was now almost completely dark, but the gorgeous white-steeple church was lit by carefully placed spotlights. It truly was a beacon in the night. My dinner companions loved the photos of the lovely church, which became lovelier as the next bottle of wine went around the table.

Five days later the Congregational Church of Grafton contacted me. Would I send more information? Of course! I had less than two weeks left before my last Sunday in Burlington. Emails zipped back and forth. The Grafton church loved my profile. I worried that they were too enthused and carefully explained I was now in conversation with two other churches. One of those churches was a devoted congregation in a wild and beautiful part of New Hampshire and the other, was, to put it bluntly, my dream church: large, wealthy, and established. It would be a positive career move for me. Both churches had contacted me within a couple of days of Don's pilgrimage to Grafton and I immediately scheduled interviews with them. Although relieved that Grafton was not "the awful church," I still needed to be clear with their eager search committee—I had not made up my mind about anything.

Within a week of hearing from them, the secretary for the Grafton Search Committee sent an exuberant email expressing excitement about the Skype interview which was to happen the next day. Her eagerness about my profile and the upcoming interview was palpable. As a way to "help me get to know them," she attached a picture of the entire congregation standing on the front steps of the church. At a glance, I thought they looked like a thriving congregation: nearly a hundred people laughing and smiling as they crowded on the steps of a church early one Sunday morning. In full sunlight. I took a harder, longer look at the photo and after a moment, picked up the phone and called Don. This enthusiastic, friendly congregation stood on the steps of the most decrepit, paint-peeling old church I had ever seen. Actually, I *had* seen it. It was the awful church. Too late though—my interview was the next day. Oh, well, I thought. I had two other solid interviews lined up at well-established churches. I didn't need Grafton anymore.

Two things: never make a life-changing decision based on a paint job and never photograph your prospective church in the soft glow of a New England sunset.

~ ~ ~ ~

Here I am, five months later, sitting in the pastor's office of the Grafton Congregational Church. The Town Common is as picturesque as ever. Outside my office window is a white picket fence that leads down a winding hill called, of course, Church Street. Everything about the town is delightful, beautiful—painted and groomed within an inch of its life. Except us—the Congregational Church. We still look as if we're standing on our last leg. But we aren't. And that's why I am here.

When I did my Skype interview with the Grafton Search Committee, I discovered the church had just finished a capital campaign, raising $360K in only a few weeks—a campaign that would address all the building issues that scared me off in the first place. This piece of knowledge—the $360K—was absolutely key to my continuing further in the interview process with the Grafton church. When I first saw the church and declared it "the awful church," I thought I was observing a church in irreversible decline. And a church in such decline tends to stay that way until an outside force acts upon it and jolts it out of its lassitude. This church had seemed so far into decline I couldn't imagine anything jolting it anywhere. Yet a congregation committed to a capital campaign was different. A capital campaign was about the only thing drastic enough—short of a wrecking ball—that could move that church out of its physical depression.

The news of the capital campaign said something else to me as well. It told me they most likely had a solid core of people willing to pledge not just their time and effort, but also their money to saving the church. That was a congregation I was willing to serve. In fact, that kind of pluck and spirit would be an honor to serve. And they sounded like a lot of fun.

In the Skype interview with the search committee, I discovered a few other things that continued my optimistic view of the church. The congregation had a thriving, justice-centered mission at its core, nearly thirty children, lots of diversity in age groups, a strong desire to become Open and Affirming, and an awesome sense of both humor and humility. In the interview I heard true satisfaction in the voices of the search committee members when I asked what they loved about their church. When I clicked off the Skype, I knew they had what I wanted. Prudence told me to do the other two interviews—especially with my dream church. But it turns out wealthy and established and prestigious isn't for me, and with the offer of a second interview, I ended my conversations with the church-of-my-dreams. It turns out the true church of my dreams has a boiler that shuts off in the coldest weather, windows that won't open, molding basement walls, and an energy for following Jesus that never quits. I am where I was meant to be.

All that said, one other big reason made me choose this church. That reason is simple: this church will grow. Grow in numbers.

Grow in spirit. Grow in mission. The desire to grow was evident in the energy of the search committee. It has continued to be evident in the cabinet meetings, in difficult building committee meetings, in worship, in Sunday school, and in the coffee shop down the street when I talk to community members about the church. It is a church on the cusp of taking off, and I want to be the pastor responsible for its launch.

About three weeks before the congregation voted to decide if I would indeed be their new minister, Peter and I met to discuss my contract, or as the United Church of Christ terms it, my "call agreement." After a fruitful negotiation in which we reached a mutually satisfying arrangement concerning my salary and benefits, we took our meeting across the town common to a quaint New England coffee shop. While sitting in the coffee shop, Peter told me he'd written a book. Immediately, he piqued my interest. I had been struggling to complete a mystery novel for several years and wondered how he did it. Especially since the word "published" was attached to his statement.

"Really?" I asked. "Tell me about it!"

He began describing his book on sales called *The Golden 120 Seconds of Every Sales Call.*

As I listened to the methods of selling and creating an environment for sales, all I could think was "this is about the church!" Finally I stopped him. "Wait a minute. This could be the church. It really could. I mean, I consider myself in sales." I hesitated. "Well, sales and service anyway." I went on to explain what I meant, "I think growing a church is about sales and I think the concepts of your book could be applied almost directly to what a pastor does to grow a church."

And at that moment, our book *Jump Start This Church!* was born. Right there in the coffee shop on the town common, nearly in the shadow of the steeple of my new church, the awful church. Which, by the way, is growing.

Chapter Two
I Don't Want to Do This

By Peter

"Why on earth would you volunteer me?" I asked. My wife Mary had just returned from a church meeting and casually told me she put forth my name to serve on the newly formed search committee.

"Because you're perfect for it," Mary said. "In fact you're exactly what they need."

Mary and I have been members of the Congregational Church of Grafton, Massachusetts, for over twenty-five years, and while she was deeply involved in the life of the church during those years, I had merely attended. In fact, for the first twenty-three and a half years of church membership I skillfully and carefully avoided getting too involved. Just thinking about Mary's news that she nominated me for the pastoral search committee, a group dedicated to finding the next pastor for our 270-year-old church, made me feel tired. I callously mused to myself, "let someone else do it."

My lack of enthusiasm grew worse when I read an email from the Church Moderator. He warned the nominated candidates about the rigor of the role, the responsibilities associated (weekly meetings), and the requirement that selected candidates be prepared for a potentially lengthy process. I read the email to Mary, concluding with: "I really don't want to do this. I'm going to send Todd a note requesting he remove my name from the list of nominees."

Her only response was "Well, if you want to, but I think you'd be great on this committee." So while I wanted to fire off that email to Todd telling him to remove my name, I couldn't bring myself to hit the "send" key. **Three weeks later, standing in front of the congregation with eight other people during our commissioning as the new search committee, the reality of this commitment hit me. Especially when the interim pastor announced that our first meeting was the next day. "You'll start at seven o'clock," he said. "And be on time. You have a lot to cover."**

Only forty minutes into our first search committee meeting, I'd had enough. When the interim pastor reviewed a monthly timeline for the search processes, I was stunned. The search couldn't possibly take that long. I broke in, "We do this in the business world all the time. If a client asked me to find, recruit, and place a Vice President of Sales for his company, and I said it would take two years, he'd tell me he was taking his business elsewhere."

Another member of the committee astutely picked up on my comment: "I completely understand where Peter is coming from," he began. Good! Vindication, I thought. Yet he continued in a direction opposite from what I hoped: "Many of us at this table have experienced what Peter is talking about, but that process is so different from hiring a pastor. This process needs to take time."

"It's a period of discernment," added another committee member. "It could easily take two years." I was overwhelmed by intense, inescapable feelings of not-wanting-to-do-this.

I felt trapped as we plodded through the rest of the meeting, mercilessly concluding after two hours and agreeing we would meet each Monday evening at 7 p.m.

I was working on a project that took me to Boston every day—a forty-five-mile drive that took almost an hour in perfect conditions. Add heavy traffic, precipitation of any kind, a single minor fender bender, solar glare, speed traps, or lengthy lines at the tolls, and the drive turned into a ninety minute one way commute, if not longer. The seven o'clock start time for our search committee meeting became increasingly difficult for me. After my repeated late arrivals, the other committee members graciously agreed to a later start time of 7:30 to accommodate my challenging commute. This was generous. Most committee members lived or worked only a few miles from the church and making the meeting even later was a sacrifice for them.

Within a few weeks we constructed our church profile and listened to church experts telling us again about the lengthy process that required patience and careful discernment. I wanted out. Once again, I decided to resign.

Too fearful to phone the committee chairperson, I sent an email explaining the challenges I faced with the role, my schedule, and my feeling of being completely overwhelmed. **I realize now that I conveniently forgot about the covenant to participate faithfully I had voiced in front of the congregation a few Sundays before.**

I sent an email to the chairperson on a Monday morning thinking my timing would give her time to communicate to the group on my behalf, and allow me to miss that evening's meeting. Isn't that something? They push out the start time of the meeting and now the guy quits.

I received a return email the following morning—a wonderful heartfelt note, but not what I wanted to read. The committee chair explained she shared my note with the other committee members (yikes!), and the consensus was that we had all made a commitment to the church. Rather than resigning, they preferred I stay on even if it meant occasionally missing a meeting.

I drafted a response reiterating my earlier position of wanting out, of needing to resign. I had every intention of sending it to her. But I didn't. Instead, I reflected for hours on the email she sent me. After my initial annoyance that she shared my note with the entire committee, I realized how meaningful her response had been. I couldn't quit.

So on we went, with me still fighting traffic to make it by 7:30.

Five months into the process the search committee began reviewing the many candidate profiles that flooded in. All the search committee experts warned us this review is a period of discernment. They didn't mention it was also heavy labor. We carefully read the profile of each candidate (about 30 pages each). Some were intriguing, others awful, and thankfully, a few were compelling. The compelling profiles led to further review and consideration followed by further engagement. Further engagement meant further discernment of the candidate, including reviewing sermons and other literary efforts. If we all felt positive about a candidate, we sent an invitation for a face-to-face interview. Sometimes further review and consideration led to disengagement, which I found painful. It's excruciating to say "no" to someone who's hoping for "yes." Importantly, the search committee had agreed we would only recommend a candidate to the congregation when we reached complete consensus.

Our first few in-person interviews resulted in a unanimous vote not to proceed.

The next candidate we interviewed, candidate John Doe, created a challenge to the committee. **After a great deal of "discernment" we were one vote short of a unanimous decision to call this candidate. A single dissenter—me. I voted "no" and threw a monkey wrench into the whole process. I** felt horrible, but I couldn't back down. I truly did not think this particular candidate was right for our congregation. The vote was eight to one. I hated being the "one."

By this time our committee had forged a caring symbiosis and mutual respect for each other, and I felt as if I put that relationship at risk. This was an emotionally jarring and contentious juncture in the search process. Our polite conversation masked underlying tension I knew I had caused.

But we were lucky. Our search committee chaplain was a true spiritual leader who kept us united and moving forward. By the following Monday evening, renewed optimism motivated us as we started digging through a new set of profiles. However, we plowed through the stacks of profiles without a mutual spark. Candidate profiles 50 through 55 were reviewed with no interest from the committee; then profiles 56-59, 60-66. Same deal. And then candidate profile 67 arrived.

Candidate 67.

Energy seemed to fill the room as each search committee member voted to proceed in gathering more information from and about candidate 67. The angst of the prior vote melted away. Perhaps we were onto something.

The vetting process led us to gather and review additional information on candidate 67, and after further discernment and review the committee voted unanimously to move to the crucial step of an interview. Due to the distance between our church and candidate 67, we elected to interview via Skype. Not as good as in-person due to its two dimensional nature, but cheaper in the long run, especially if we ended up rejecting the candidate.

While three of the nine committee members weren't able to attend the interview, the other six were enthused about the prospect of speaking with candidate 67. As I had been the lone dissenter in the vote to proceed with candidate John Doe, I was especially sensitive to the process of discernment and my responsibility as part of that covenant. The process involved researching this candidate beyond the information provided in the profile.

Upon reflection, I realized my lack of confidence in candidate John Doe centered around the issue of church growth. Our church was in desperate need of renewal and rejuvenation. I kept remembering the video-taped sermon of candidate 35. She discussed the fact that more than 5,000 churches close every year. I knew we needed a pastor who would grow the church, and I didn't feel John Doe was that person. But being the only dissenter was a lonely place, and despite my attempts to stay committed to my decision, the response of some of my fellow committee members resulted in two nights of lost sleep. I found some degree of solace by the third night when I acknowledged that while John Doe wasn't right for our church, John Doe would be right for another church. We needed someone who could renew growth and energy.

> Our church was in desperate need of renewal and rejuvenation. We needed someone who could renew growth and energy.

I did research in preparation for our Skype interview with candidate 67. I liked her on paper and felt she was worthy of the time the committee would invest.

I was both anxious and excited about the upcoming interview. I was ready to logically and methodically evaluate candidate 67, Reverend Jane Willan, in a pragmatic manner that would lead to a list of carefully considered reasons why we should continue her candidacy or disengage from it.

But I wasn't prepared for what actually occurred as the interview got underway. Rather than feeling like an integral part of the process, as the Skype interview commenced I felt more like a vessel for something predestined to happen. Within thirty seconds, I felt an overpowering belief that she was the one.

This feeling was so quick, urgent, and real that I could barely consciously consider it. I was "told" she was the one. It was like the sensation of touching a hot stove and recoiling your hand from the stove top just slightly before your brain can process the pain message.

I knew this candidate was what the church needed, wanted, and frankly, had-to-have in order to grow. Of course I also knew that my vote was only one of nine, and that the entire congregation would need to vote in acceptance to make it official. We were a long way from that point. At the conclusion of the interview we all felt energy, enthusiasm, and celebration in the committee room. Candidate Reverend Jane Willan could be the one!

We shared our enthusiasm over the next few days with the other members of the search committee which led to a real in-person interview at my house. Mary did a wonderful job making our house welcome, coordinating an excellent meal, and taking the time to show Jane's husband Don around the parsonage and church. Mary did all this with graciousness and generosity, as though she instinctively knew Jane was the right candidate as well.

As I drove Jane back to the church to meet Don and Mary, I was struck by the incredible sense of energy and excitement I felt about the evening. Similar to the experience thirty seconds into the Skype interview, I knew this was right. Of course, I couldn't convey much of that to Jane, since the committee members hadn't met alone. But it was difficult to mask my enthusiasm over the direction the process was heading. **I felt Jane would be a magnet for our church and, as a fellow search committee member put it, "fill the pews again."**

When the search committee met the next evening, the committee chair asked if we were ready to take a vote. My heart pounded. Until all the votes had been cast, I couldn't be sure. I remembered that in the voting process for candidate John Doe, the first six votes were all in favor, creating significant momentum and energy in the room—until I cast my dissenting vote.

This time the voting occurred quickly and enthusiastically, which was good because my heart was about to explode. Nine voted in favor of offering the call, no one against. It was done. The committee chairwoman placed the congratulatory call to Jane and offered the position. Tears fell from the chairwoman's eyes as Jane told her she "enthusiastically accepted."

A few weeks later the congregation voted unanimously to approve Reverend Jane Willan as the next pastor of our church. The most important building block to growing our church was in place.

I was so glad I hadn't said "No" to Mary's nomination.

I was so glad I hadn't said "No" to the moderator.

I was so glad I hadn't said "I quit" (a second time) to the search committee chairperson

I was so glad I said "No" to candidate John Doe.

And, most importantly, I was glad everyone in the Church said "yes" to Reverend Jane.

~ ~ ~ ~

Why this book? Why now?

By trade, I am a sales professional. I started my career selling $8 advertisements in a small weekly newspaper in Vermont. My sales career progressed to selling radio advertising, which led me into the world of consulting, which led to my book *The Golden 120 Seconds of Every Sales Call.* I have since started my own sales consulting practice and work with wonderful organizations and salespeople in companies large and small. My clients include salespeople with no experience and salespeople with up to forty years of experience.

In the first of our many "coffee meetings," I described this book concept to Reverend Jane. She surprised me by saying she'd like to read it. I was even more shocked when, 24 hours after giving her the book, she responded by saying, "How about writing a book together? The church needs this."

My business experience in the secular world tells me that many elements of good selling absolutely apply to growing or "selling" our churches. In fact, **an argument could be made that Jesus himself was an excellent salesman (I acknowledge this could be a contentious issue).** The underlying theme of this book is that if candidate #35 was correct and 5,000 churches close every year, then we need to do something. We must view the urgent problem of dying churches with fresh eyes.

This book is all about that fresh look. A collaboration between a sales expert and an effective church leader, *Jump Start This Church!* embraces church growth from a new perspective.

We hope this book will trigger dialogue and action for churches throughout the world. *Jump Start This Church!* isn't another book written from inside the walls of the church by a discouraged member of the clergy. Rather, it's a collaboration of the secular and religious viewpoint; from outside as well as in.

If we can keep only one of those 5,000 churches from closing, we will have succeeded.

Chapter Three

*The First 120 Seconds
(Actually, You May Not Have That Long)*

By Peter

Twenty five years ago, Mary made an announcement that would change our lives. "I've found the one!" she exclaimed. "I found our new church. The building is beautiful and old; it is so New England! The pastor's awesome! The pews are filled and there are lots of kids!" Mary continued, "I felt like I'd come home. They invited me to sing in the choir. Everyone was so nice. Coffee-hour was packed."

Mary was sold.

A week later, I was sold too. I stood at the back of the church gently rocking Hilary (our six month old) as Mary sat up front with the choir. A few weeks later we became members of the church.

Today, we are still faithful, and involved members of the same church. Mary has sung in the church choir since day one and I am now the moderator. This spring we will participate in our 26th stewardship campaign, where members are asked to contribute financially to support the church. Twenty six years of membership triggered by a single positive experience! Not a bad return for the church I'd say.

All this was based on the initial connection—an interaction I refer to as *The First Golden 120 Seconds*.

Finding our church happened because Mary undertook the project of visiting local and nearby churches, while I stayed home, refusing to participate. Luckily for us she was adamant about finding a church home for our growing family.

While not interested in going on the church visit circuit, I was interested in hearing her feedback when she came home from these Sunday morning prospective church visits. Her commentary generally fell into one of two categories. The first was something along the lines of "No, that's not the one; I'd never go back there." The other had the sentiment of "Well, it was okay, I guess I'll give it another shot. Maybe you'll come with me if I go there again?" But I knew in my heart if she wasn't moved enough to feel like returning on her own, then the church wasn't a good candidate.

> A single Sunday morning gave each church an opportunity to acquire us as members. Only one church "sold" itself to Mary, a customer who was actively shopping for a new church.

In all those negative experiences, and the one positive visit, a single Sunday morning gave each church an opportunity to acquire us as members. Only one church "sold" itself to Mary, a customer who was actively shopping for a new church.

As a professional salesperson, I believe parish ministry incorporates many of the elements of professional selling. As Reverend Jane said in Chapter One, "I am a salesperson."

And as Mary touted in her energetic review of the winning church "The pastor's awesome!"

I think the pastor plays a huge role in the sales process. Of course I realize being a good pastor includes a multitude of requirements that have nothing to do with sales, but for this discussion, I'm focusing on personal qualities that are related to selling.

The importance of the initial interaction is underscored by the link between growing a church by increasing its membership. Positive growth curves develop when churches are able to attract visitors in the first place, and then bring them back. The pastor and lay leadership must be sensitive to the cruel fact that they have only a single opportunity to make this happen. One shot to trigger a 25-year-plus membership relationship. That is sales pressure!

Conversely, if the potential new member leaves without returning, look what you've lost. Five thousand churches a year are closing. Are some of these failures due to the pastor's lack of sensitivity and accountability for nurturing current members and gathering new members?

Definitely!

So, what happens during those golden 120 seconds? What needs to happen? I believe it comes down to three elements:

♦ What the pastor says during the initial presentation,

♦ What the pastor conveys through body language and non-verbal communication,

♦ And finally the "customer experience," or what it's like for someone to enter the church, sit in the pews, and absorb the proceedings.

Let's examine each of these interactions, starting with the pastor's initial welcoming statement and preparation for the Sunday service.

Initial presentation: As the pastor, you've written the sermon, a deacon has placed a glass of fresh water on the lectionary for you, and the choir is in place ready to begin singing. You look over the congregation and notice a couple of visitors sitting by themselves. These are people who've taken the big step of walking through unfamiliar doors on Sunday morning, probably feeling a bit nervous. Congratulations, you have prospects in the building!

As you went over the sermon, did you practice your opening statement? Have you looked in the mirror while reciting it? Are you able to deliver your welcome while making eye contact with parishioners and visitors alike—and without looking at notes?

From the moment you step into the sanctuary, you are being sized-up by newcomers and your parishioners who log subconscious responses at a frenetic pace. Things like "Wow, he seems nice." or "Strikes me as confident" "She has an air about her" "Nice smile" or "She doesn't look very happy" "Boy, his hair is a mess" "He looks tired and hunched over."

Like it or not, that's what happens. Talk about pressure. To help ease that pressure, I recommend you think like a salesperson as you prepare for the initial welcome statement.

Why are you excited about this service?

Why are you excited to see the people are in the pews?

What will they experience today?

What are you thankful for?

Why are you welcoming visitors and long term members?

As I tell sales teams: "Be prepared by creating an opening script or a series of bullet points, and then memorize it." You'll be able to deliver a compelling introduction that creates momentum and energy. Visitors and members will feel good about making the decision to attend your church on Sunday.

Nonverbal communication: Preparation for this first golden 120 seconds also requires sensitivity to the power of body language and non-verbal communication skills. Your best efforts to present a compelling message are wasted if people are distracted by your mannerisms or turned off by your appearance. You want everyone to focus on your selling messages, especially the vital first two minutes of your presentation. You can't afford the luxury of having their attention diverted. If they miss the impact of these first two minutes, you'll have a lot of ground to make up.

An aura of professionalism gives you a strong advantage before you open your mouth. The unspoken message conveyed by your physical appearance and approach will influence a visitor's opinion about your church on a subliminal, unconscious level. In sales terms, you can "blow the sale" before uttering a single word of your sermon.

Prospects buy from a specific sales person because they believe he or she will be "good to work with" and because they have rapport. I've witnessed many elements of body language that up-ended sales presentations and sent prospects flocking to pursue the seller's competitors. We've all heard stories from people in a buying situation who say "I just didn't feel comfortable with that guy. Did you see his fingernails? His shoes were a mess. And he didn't listen to me. He didn't hear a word I said."

The same thing is true of church growth situations. Therefore, I recommend you pay attention to the following elements of non-verbal communication at every service.

♦ Fingernails

Trimmed and clean: Nothing sucks the momentum out of a presentation like ten chewed-to-a-crisp fingernails. After all, you'll be performing baptisms! Also, keep fingers out of your mouth, your nose, and off your face during your sermon.

♦ Hands

The use of hands in a sermon is almost as important as how baseball players use their hands in fielding their positions. Keep your hands visible; avoid having them out of view. Use hands to emphasize points, but other than that, try to keep them still.

◆ Handshake

This is a vital interaction you'll have with prospective members—and you'd better get it right. How you shake hands says a lot about you. If your hand is wet and clammy, wipe it off. If that never seems to work, try relaxation techniques like visualization before you meet visitors. Do not squeeze with a vise-like grip, but don't let your hand go limp as a dead fish either.

◆ Hair

Your hair should be well groomed and out of your eyes. Don't touch or comb it in front of a prospect. Have your hair professionally cut in a fashionable, but not outlandish, style. Men, don't leave hair growing in the wrong places—down your neck, inside your nose, or untamed eyebrows.

◆ Eyes

Good eye contact reveals confidence and control. But don't overdo it and stare your parishioners down. That's scary. You should look people in the eyes for emphasis, to show integrity, and most importantly, when you ask for something. And when you're in the pulpit—you are often asking.

◆ Attire

Wear professional or business casual clothing, as appropriate. Your clothing should fit well and be appropriately ironed and fresh looking. Get rid of that ten-year-old suit and baggy pants. Women, try to find a pleasing balance between too sexy and overly prim.

◆ Shoes

Keep your footwear clean, polished, properly soled, and nicely laced. Invest in at least one pair of quality shoes, because cheap shoes are easy to spot. If you follow these simple rules people may never notice your shoes. If you don't, they will.

♦ Standing Position
Stand upright and authoritative—appearing engaged in a friendly, cordial manner, but also ready to handle anything that comes along.

♦ Collateral
Have on hand a brochure, a one-page description, or articles about your church. Give these handouts to visitors who seem interested.

These items are simple to accomplish, yet any one of them could become an issue. **Don't handicap yourself by neglecting the easy things.** None of them will turn a bad sermon into a good one, but they each have the potential to ruin a good sermon—and you may never know what happened.

With practice, your preparation for service and your ability to use sales elements to help grow your church can become valuable assets for you and your congregation.

The customer experience: Beyond the look and feel of your church lies the critical issue of how visitors are treated during the service. The welcome they receive speaks volumes to visitors about how we feel about them, and how happy we are to have them join us. You don't want to overwhelm people, but at the same time, you don't want to neglect them or be slow to respond to their requests. Treat them the way you'd want to be treated. Consider the negative effect of making visitors stand up to be recognized (never do this), or failing to speak to them after the service—a perfect way to make sure they never come back.

By remaining sensitive, you can synthesize a flawlessly executed initial impression for your visitors. That all-important first 120-seconds is the springboard for the rest of your service. How you present yourself and how the church presents itself will set the tone for the church experience of your visitors. And that experience will decide whether or not they return.

Of course you'll also apply these concepts to your congregation during individual meetings, cabinet and committee meetings you attend, and all church activities. And let's not forget the people you meet in neighborhood coffee shops, sporting events, and other community activities. Seriousness about growing a church requires seriousness of preparation for all these interactions.

Let's review what you accomplished in that 120 seconds and why it's important to achieve flawless execution at this critical juncture. You've established your church as friendly, welcoming, and inviting. In the sales world clients buy, whenever possible, from people they like. Likewise, people choose a church with a pastor they like and a congregation with which they feel comfortable. They need to feel positive about the person with whom they'll be working—the pastor. If you let these ideas become the foundation for growing your church, you'll make it easy for visitors to say, "I just found my new church!"

Jane's Commentary

I reluctantly agree with Peter. The first 120 seconds (and he is right—you may not even have that long) are key, and a pastor should be ready to make the most of those critical two minutes. Why am I reluctant to agree with Peter on this point? Because it's frightening to acknowledge that the impression a pastor makes is so crucial. It scares me to think of the times I may have "blown it" in my personal presentation to a new person. Church people—especially clergy—want to say the pastor isn't the most important element to church growth. But clearly, the pastor is absolutely central, and how that individual presents can make or break the return of a visitor. We would rather give the credit for church growth (or church decline) to everyone from the parishioners to the Holy Spirit, but at the end of the day—it's the pastor.

Making it Happen Worksheet

Create a checklist for the first 120 seconds that works for you:

1. _____

2. _____

3. _____

4. _____

5. _____

Try your checklist next Sunday. What would you add? What didn't work?

1. _____

2. _____

3. _____

4. _____

5. _____

Chapter Four

Throwing Out Needlepoint Jesus

By Jane

I was late for my meeting and I hate being late. I had left home at 5:00 that morning and had driven four long hours across the endless cornfields of southeast Iowa, only to miss the beginning of the workshop. Suddenly, out of the empty cornfields appeared a welcome sign for my destination, and shortly thereafter I saw a church steeple. I quickly turned left into the church drive and followed the arrow that said *Church Parking.* I kept driving past the church building where I could see the crowd already gathering inside, probably grabbing all the best seats and the last of the coffee and doughnuts. I continued following the arrows past a playground, then a prayer garden. Surely I would reach the parking lot soon.

Finally, I turned into an area designated for visitors. I think I was parked about a hundred yards from the church door. The back door. Which had a sign that read: Use Side Door Only. As I hurried around the corner of the church building and up the steep sidewalk to the closest side door, I could hear the applause from the gathered clergy as they welcomed the guest speaker.

Tugging on the handle of the door, I found it was locked. Frustrated, I peered through a small window. The room on the other side of the door was dark and looked like it was used for storage.

"Over here!" a voice called. I turned to see a colleague who attended this particular church holding open a door for me. I hurried toward him, down a short walk and up a set of steps. The correct side door. The only entrance into the large church.

Rule number one of growing your church: If you want people to come, don't make getting into the building a mystery.

Your church's physical presentation, from basement to bell tower, is an indication of whether or not it will grow. A welcoming church has doors that open, well-lit hallways, and entranceways that make you want to enter. Do you want your church to grow? Then get rid of clutter, cultivate a contemporary aura, and make sure it smells good. Your physical space is essential to growth.

> Your church's physical presentation, from basement to bell tower, is an indication of whether or not it will grow.

This chapter contains everything you need to know about creating a physical space that will pull people in and make them want to stay.

Look at your church with the fresh eyes of a visitor. In the first week of my new parish here in Grafton, I felt an immediate need to do something about the front entrance of the church. It is an old New England church with a tall steeple on the village green and entering its massive front doors gave me a certain sense of the sacred. It was a dramatic space with carpet of deep burgundy, old polished wood and gentle lighting. But after a moment, the beauty of the entrance was entirely lost in the clutter of food pantry donations, stacks of crumpled church bulletins, old hymnals, tattered Bibles, abandoned coats hanging askew on a coat rack, and strangely, a large wooden door leaning against the wall.

Thursday night during my first week as pastor of the Grafton church, while the choir practiced in the sanctuary I began cleaning. The leftover bulletins, hymnbooks, and Bibles were easy enough to deal with (dumpster or storage). The food donations were quickly organized and coats were simply hung up in the vestry. The abandoned wooden door proved more difficult. The door was the first thing visitor saw when entering the church. The door was as tall as me and might have weighed more. I called one of the trustees and asked him why an old door stood in the narthex. I thought there must be a good reason and I just couldn't figure it out.

"I don't know, Pastor," he said.

"How long has it been there?" I asked.

"As far as I know, it's been there since I joined the church."

"When was that?"

"Not that long. Maybe about eight years ago."

We grow immune to the look of our own churches and miss the clutter, dirty carpets, and the calendar that shows the very busy December we had last year. We might not even ask why a door stands leaning against a wall for nearly a decade.

To a person entering the church for the first time, this is all a big deal. Everything they see within the first few seconds sends a message. The message could be one of life and hope, optimism, and energy. Or it could be the message that your church is run by people who barely care what goes on. They care so little that they let junk pile up and the place starts to resemble a badly organized storage space, not a community of faith engaged in the business of changing the world.

By the way, two enthusiastic choir members came to my rescue and we pitched the door into the dumpster that very night. Not a single church member missed it or even wondered where it was and the narthex no longer resembles the remains of an unsuccessful tag sale. I find the dark of night a good time to visit the church dumpster.

You will need to be fearless in your efforts to clean and de-clutter. Cheerfully ignore the protests of all those who don't like your changes. Redecorating, throwing out trash, and de-cluttering your church is a first and crucial step to growing your church. It may also be the most controversial thing you do in your ministry. You will encounter more disapproval about decorating than anything theological. I recently told my church in a sermon that I was pretty sure Jesus was married and the wedding at Cana was his own wedding. That radical statement got almost no response, but the new colors with which I had just painted my office (a burnt yellow with a plum accent wall) were widely discussed for weeks.

> You will need to be fearless in your efforts to clean and de-clutter.

As pastor, you will have to lead the crusade for changing church décor. My advice is to avoid assigning a committee and don't ask for permission. Simply take the needlepoint picture of Jesus off the wall and toss it in the dumpster (if it makes you nervous to throw Jesus into the dumpster, stash it in a hidden spot). Paint the wall and hang up a fresh, new print from an artsy website before anyone has time to call a meeting of the Pastor Parish Relations committee. Did you go into ministry to be afraid of annoyed old ladies? No. Did you love every word of *The Courage to Be*? Yes. So read it again and keep cleaning.

The reason a pastor needs to take church décor seriously is that a church gives off its own energy. When a new person walks into your building for the first time, you want that person to recognize your church's energy. In order to portray energy, each room of your church, from the smallest Sunday school room to the front of the sanctuary, must have a focal point. A focal point is the first thing that people see when they enter a room. In other words, the focal point is the element or elements that immediately demonstrate the room's true function.

Ask yourself, what is the focal point of the entryway that people see the moment they walk into the church? What is the focal point of the fellowship hall? What is the focal point of the sanctuary?

In a previous church, we had a display of black and white photographs of each pastor dating back to 1884. Those pictures were the first thing you saw when you walked in. Although it was a neat piece of their history, as a focal point it failed. The old photos told visitors the purpose of the church was that of museum. Yet we were not a museum by any stretch of the imagination. It was a congregation deeply engaged in social justice and was a growing center of the local community. It's good to celebrate the past, but not in the front lobby. Does your opening space give off the energy you want it to? Or does it make you want to take a nap? Does it make you want to go somewhere that has energy—like the coffee shop down the street?

Coffee shops learned a decade ago that presentation is everything. Consider what you like about your favorite coffee shop. Mine focuses on my comfort and relaxation. When I walk in, I'm greeted with warm colors, the smell of coffee, comfortable chairs, inviting tables, and people clicking away on keyboards as they visit with each other. All good coffee shops now have internet access, and so should your church. Being online at a moment's notice is now an expected part of our world. Like it or not, people text during sermons, check their email, and post on Instagram.

We live in a world where church is a choice—one of many, many choices in a frantically busy world. If the church doesn't present as alive and active and significant then we will never get anyone to walk through our doors or return after an initial visit. And frankly, we won't deserve anyone.

Peter's Commentary

In the business and sales world the term "out-of-the-box" experience refers to the initial impression a purchased product offers. Particularly startling about Reverend Jane's commentary is that much of what she references occurred in my church! The church I've been coming to for twenty-six years. Was I in such a daze when I entered the church for all those years? Somehow, I didn't notice these things. Perhaps this situation was similar to my home, where I grew accustomed to things that needed my attention and they miraculously morphed over time into a state of normalcy. Perhaps I felt so comfortable in my relationship with my church that I didn't scrutinize these things.

But I must also consider the next level of my absence of scrutiny. For the past two years I'd been involved in the church as a deacon, then a member of the search committee, and then as moderator. I was acutely aware of lighting and sound issues in the church because my mother-in-law, who recently moved to our area and joined the church, was challenged by trying to hear. Yet, I managed to overlook all the examples cited by Reverend Jane. I find that startling.

A few months before calling Reverend Jane, the interim pastor and his wife came to our house one Sunday for lunch. The pastor's wife is a wonderful, thoughtful, caring, and candid woman—someone who says it like it is. As we enjoyed dessert she told about a friend of hers who attended our church two Sundays earlier. She explained that her friend is an expert in church infrastructure issues, with a particular focus on the appearance of a church and whether or not a visitor would be inclined to return after an initial visit.

In the friend's informal report, she adamantly declared our church, the church we loved, did not create a welcoming initial appearance. Her commentary was something along the lines of "Is this church doing okay?" Our dilapidated appearance did not represent the dynamic people in the congregation.

She cited such issues as peeling paint in the entryway and rips in the leather-faced doors leading into the sanctuary. (I've seen those doors hundreds of times and never noticed. Yikes!). The front doors were heavy and difficult to open, and she noticed a rusting mirror in the ladies bathroom. "Go to Home Depot and buy a new mirror for $30 for heaven's sake,'" she said. And we had peeling plaster over the pulpit.

Her feedback was both wonderfully candid and embarrassing.

Upon further reflection, I now wonder how many visitors (those who actually made it through the heavy doors) were negatively influenced right away by one, two, or more of these physical dynamics. Perhaps they never came back.

While even a single visitor lost is one too many, I suspect over the years we lost tens, if not hundreds, of prospective members.

Making it Happen Worksheet

Convene a committee of lay leaders to take a tour. Scrutinize each of the following areas in your church, noting what looks tired, what needs to be repaired, and what can be brightened. Don't forget to notice clutter. Make a list using the following.

Front Entrance:

1. _____

2. _____

3. _____

Side Entrance:

1. _____

2. _____

3. _____

Back Entrance:

1. _____

2. _____

3. _____

Narthex:

1. _____

2. _____

3. _____

Sanctuary:

1. _____

2. _____

3. _____

Fellowship Hall:

1. _____

2. _____

3. _____

Offices:

1. _____

2. _____

3. _____

Classrooms:

1. _____

2. _____

3. _____

Kitchen:

1. _____

2. _____

3. _____

Parking Lot:

1. _____

2. _____

3. _____

Bathrooms:

1. _____

2. _____

3. _____

Other:

1. _____

2. _____

3. _____

Then, prioritize the needed improvements. We suggest a Top Ten List. And remember, be fearless!

1. _____

2. _____

3. _____

4. _____

5. _____

6. _____

7. _____

8. _____

9. _____

10. _____

Chapter Five
In Jane We Trust

By Peter

Our plane sat motionless on the tarmac. The low idle of the engines provided barely adequate ventilation and heat. The flight attendants stood motionless at their stations. We weren't leaving anytime soon.

Detroit weather wasn't cooperating. Steady snowfall and temperatures in the low twenties meant that each departing flight required de-icing prior to take off. And then, once de-iced, we had a tight window of time in which to take off, as departure depended on how recently the two serviceable runways had been plowed. This was an epic dance of human beings, sophisticated machines, and the whims of mother nature.

I sat squashed into my window seat watching the snow fall and listening to the hum of the engines. The traveler next to me, having donned his noise cancelling headphones, had apparently drifted to sleep. His left elbow encroached into my "airspace" to the left of the armrest that separated us, and his left knee encroached into my space to the left of the imaginary line splitting us below the seat. I was beginning to feel slightly claustrophobic.

How long were we going to be here?

How long could I stay in this very tight space without going crazy?

I was drifting from "safety first" to "I just want to get out of here!"

Shortly thereafter, much to my relief, a de-icing truck maneuvered into position next to our plane. I watched as they began working. The anticipated melting of the ice on the plane was also melting away my angst and restlessness. My window seat was over the wing, giving me a great view of the proceedings.

The large truck was positioned by the driver—dressed in big winter parka, ski mask, and thick gloves—just in front of the left wing. Up in the enclosed bucket compartment perched about 30 feet in the air sat his partner, similarly dressed, with his hands on the triggers of the high pressure hoses, preparing to release the de-icing fluid onto the wings.

The action began!

Red fluid splashed onto the wings and up into the windows; and as it dripped down the window and cleared my view. The process took three minutes. The truck then reversed about ten yards. The driver and hose operator looked to their left as another member of the grounds crew approached the wing.

This third member of the team had the same hat and coat as the other two, but not the gloves, which was surprising in the snow and twenty degree air.

No gloves! Was he crazy?

Turns out quite the contrary. In fact he was an important member of the crew; perhaps the most vital member.

With the driver and the hose operator focused intently on his every move, the third man proceeded to run his ungloved fingers down the front surface of the wing, checking how well the de-icing fluid had penetrated the ice that had caked along the tip of the wing. At infrequent intervals he stepped back from the wing and signaled to the bucket operator to re-spray smaller sections of the wing. He then did the same on the reverse side of the wing.

This element of human touch was in stark contrast to the state-of-the-art electronics and sophistication all around me on the plane.

It was fascinating that this multi-million dollar ultramodern airplane with 200-plus people on board wasn't going anywhere until the "touch test" had been done by the ground crew technician. And it was his call—the touch from his ungloved hand would determine whether this plane was safe to fly or would stay grounded.

What an awesome responsibility.

This revelation shifted me far away mentally from the confines of my seat, and I began reflecting on how this scene was an allegory for church growth. Just as the plane wouldn't take off until this guy checked the wings with his bare hands, a church doesn't grow until the pastor quite literally gets her hands dirty.

> Just as the plane wouldn't take off until this guy checked the wings with his bare hands, a church doesn't grow until the pastor quite literally gets her hands dirty.

This means clearing out the old, transforming the new, and leaving her imprint on the infrastructure of the building. The call to action of clearing out signifies the transformation necessary to prepare for and embrace the future. It signifies the leadership position of the pastor necessary to fuel change and growth. It also demonstrates to the membership "we're moving forward." And finally, it symbolizes that being tied to the past is not an option and modernization and updating are vital ingredients for moving the church to the next stage—that is, moving from where it is today to where it's going tomorrow.

Our church had gone through seventeen years with little physical transformation. The place was tired. And, with each year that went by, I think the congregation grew tired also. This collective exhaustion then manifested itself in reduced attendance on Sundays. The church was losing energy. Ice on the wings was grounding us.

After the technician completed checking the front and rear parts of the wing, he gave a thumbs up to his crew mates and the truck moved to the next plane in line. Three minutes later the red fluid on the wings turned a bright shade of green, indicating its highest point of safety; two minutes later the captain announced, "We've been cleared for departure. Flight attendants please take your seats for takeoff."

We were on our way! "In the manual ice checker we trust," I told myself.

If a church is to grow, we must encourage and trust the pastor to check the ice, and freeze her hands to clear us for takeoff. In our church, shortly after her arrival, Reverend Jane made the decision that the tired picture of Jesus given by a church member years earlier needed to go.

Our church is growing.

"In Jane We Trust."

Jane's Commentary

I like what Peter is saying here, but I might phrase it differently. I would summarize his chapter in these words: "The pastor must show no fear." No fear of getting her hands dirty. No fear of taking a stand. No fear of herself as boss. If the pastor repeatedly hesitates to take the gloves off and touch the ice, nothing will ever change. The church will never grow. But most pastors seem afraid to do just that.

To overcome the fear of taking charge, a pastor must trust her own instincts (and I believe the church will begin to trust in the pastor) as she starts to become an agent of change.

And believe it or not, in a church, the smallest change can set off a firestorm of anxiety and protest. Consequently, without a certain level of trust in yourself, you'll never de-ice anything. In our churches today, at least the mainline Protestant churches, pastors routinely and systematically avoid initiating the steps that would lead to true transformation. Unfortunately for their churches, growth depends on transformation.

In my parish in Iowa we were on a steep hill atop a bluff overlooking the Mississippi River. Our church was perched partway up the steep hill and another church was at the top of the hill. At one time the "top of the hill church" was the premier church of the town. It had over six hundred members, a thriving youth program, and was everything a growing, vibrant church embodied. When I began as pastor at my church, the church at the top of the hill was down to less than fifty members, most of whom were over the age of 70. This decline happened in the span of two or three generations. They had gone from 600 members to 50 members in less than 30 years. The building itself was still beautiful—huge with lovely architecture, a breath-taking sanctuary, numerous Sunday school rooms, and a huge, industrial kitchen. Yet, it echoed with emptiness. What happened? As I understand it, the congregation had some difficult but powerful members (what congregation doesn't?) and these people hired passive, amenable pastors. In other words, no one who was ever going to throw out the needlepoint picture of Jesus. After a long series of these pastors, everyone was gone.

You might ask, "Why would people who really loved their church jump ship due to a poor pastor?" Because leadership is everything. If just one of those pastors had stepped up and truly led the congregation—stood up to the difficult people, insisted on change, and forced transformation—I believe that church could be thriving today. Instead, they experienced three decades of passive leadership, of letting things slide. As Peter might say, the ice on the wings took over. Their plane was permanently grounded.

Peter writes that transformation in a stagnant church only happens, physically and emotionally, when the church recognizes and supports the leadership position of the pastor. He says this support "is necessary to fuel change and growth." He is right. But I would add that each pastor must have a sense of personal authority and cannot be afraid to exert this authority. If you are passive, your church leaders will either treat you as such or get fed up and leave.

In our liberal, mainline churches, the authority of the pastor is no longer expected or possibly even welcomed. For some reason, pastors in this generation do not seem to feel at all comfortable exerting authority of any kind, as if personal authority is somehow wrong or distasteful. The attitude seems to be that if we're truly good pastors, we won't need to

> If you are passive, your church leaders will either treat you as such or get fed up and leave.

ever be the boss. Further, as pastors we aren't taught to believe in ourselves as figures of influence and clout; instead, we're taught to trust in God, to pray, to empower others. Unfortunately this approach can result in a passive style of leadership.

And over time, it will diminish the parish.

Making it Happen Worksheet

This worksheet is for you, the pastor.

In a quiet, reflective moment, identify the ten most important changes you want to make, and would make, regardless of how concerned you feel about proposing them. Just list your ideas and ignore how hard it might be to accomplish them:

1. _____

2. _____

3. _____

4. _____

5. _____

6. _____

7. _____

8. _____

9. _____

10. _____

Chapter Six

Don't be Afraid to Fire the Staff

By Jane

I watched in horror as Dorothy grabbed the spoon from the homeless person's hand and tossed it onto the counter. Dots of homemade chili splattered the wall. "This is not how you make chili!" Dorothy, chair of the Kitchen Committee, picked up a salt container and liberally shook it over the crock pot, then replaced the lid with a loud bang. The gentleman who'd been tending the chili drifted away, and as I recall, I never saw him again.

Our church had begun hosting a soup kitchen and Dorothy, who had reigned over the kitchen for nearly forty years, adamantly opposed the idea. The church board however, unanimously voted to establish a soup kitchen and since they were the final trump card in our church's governance, our new soup kitchen was a done deal—no matter how much Dorothy disliked it.

Every Tuesday evening about 100 people arrived at the church for a free meal. Sounds great, doesn't it? An event so inherently Christ-like it's hard to argue against. But Dorothy argued.

Constantly. And when her complaining couldn't stop the soup kitchen, she showed up every night to "supervise." What she really did was intimidate, insult, and spread bad energy on what was otherwise an exciting and meaningful moment in the church's growth and outreach.

As pastor, I felt frustrated and helpless. There was no talking with Dorothy. The Pastor Parish Relations Committee was afraid of her (another topic for another book). The board seemed puzzled by my concern. They reminded me that Dorothy had run the kitchen for forty years and was the only person who knew how to order supplies. And so I did the only thing I could do. I fired her. Done. Gone. No longer a kitchen lady. And I finally had to tell her she could not enter the kitchen for one year.

Sound harsh? It was. Did I have to deal with several unhappy church members? Definitely.

But I knew it was either fire Dorothy or lose a thriving outreach program that was in keeping with the church's mission and instrumental in growing the church. That was the choice I faced. Twelve years later the soup kitchen, called Open Table, is still flourishing and provides close to 5000 meals a year. I heard that Dorothy joined the Lutherans down the street. Had I allowed her to stay as the chair of the kitchen, I would have had far less conflict to deal with and in the short term my life would have been easier. But the church's overall health would have suffered and any chance for growth would have been blocked.

Don't be afraid to fire the staff, and that includes life-long kitchen ladies.

Staff is a little different in the church than in the corporate world. In a traditional business, staff means people who are paid to do what they do. In a church, especially the small to medium-sized church, staff usually includes one or two paid employees and several volunteers who chair committees or run boards. An example of paid staff would be the sexton or perhaps the church secretary. Unpaid staff would be the Moderator or the Chair of the Board of Christian Education. In this chapter, I use the word *staff* to identify both paid people and unpaid volunteers who are acknowledged leaders in the church. In my mind, all are staff and all have to be evaluated by the pastor. The litmus test for whether or not they remain on your staff should be their level of commitment to church growth.

I have often wished that when starting at a new church, a pastor could model a president assuming the oval office. The present Cabinet leaves and the president comes in with an entirely new group of employees entirely suited to his goals. In a church you don't get to fire the staff. In fact, you really don't want to. In every church I have gone to, I've inherited an extraordinarily talented staff and volunteers. But always one or two of them don't work out. Why? Because they are unable to change with the demands of a growing church, and that attitude soon becomes obvious

How do you know when a staff member isn't going to help grow the church?

Staff members who quickly begin complaining they don't like the "look" of the new congregation may not be good candidates for empowering a church to grow. A growing congregation inevitably starts to look different—especially if a commitment to diversity is a priority. If your present staff doesn't like this "new" congregation, they will manifest their discomfort in ways that will be communicated to the new people. In a past church of mine, the nominating committee refused—in a very passive way—to nominate anyone to a committee or board who had not been a member of the church for at least 10 years. In this particular church, the same people were doing all the same work and burn-out was rampant. Church energy and activity was at an all-time low. At the same time, many new people had joined the church and when several possible names emerged for positions of leadership, I couldn't convince the nominating committee to bring in the new people.

However, "firing" the nominating committee wasn't the best solution at the time. Instead, I both increased the role of the committee members and at the same time, added new members. I personally selected the new members of the committee so they were people comfortable with growth and excited about the new people in church. Slowly our boards and committees began to fill with the energy new members inevitably bring.

Another time to fire the staff is when they don't support you as pastor. This lack of pastoral support will be obvious to new people and keep the church from moving forward. Growing a church involves much more than just inviting and sustaining members. It's also about creating a cohesive, unified church body with interesting and effective programs, worship, and outreach. New members, particularly young people, won't visit or stay with churches that are not *doing* something to change the world. So if your present staff refuses to support your ideas for developing new programs, improving the worship service,

if your present staff is locked into the way things have always been, you won't grow your church. In fact, your church probably won't even be around in ten years.

or bringing in dynamic guest speakers—then you will never grow. You need staff members who support change and don't immediately tell you to hold back.

However, when I say support, I don't mean you want staff members who agree to everything without offering feedback. I recently proposed an idea to my stewardship chair and treasurer. I thought this change would make stewardship easier for our present members and less confusing for new members. Both the chair and treasurer disagreed with me and offered good reasons why my brilliant idea wouldn't work. And they were right. Both of these people are competent and I've grown to trust them. Disagreement doesn't mean lack of support, especially if it leads to healthy dialogue.

Just remember—if your present staff is locked into the way things have always been, you won't grow your church. In fact, your church probably won't even be around in ten years.

Here's another good reason to cultivate staff members who are committed to growth and eliminate those who impede growth: the act of welcoming has a trickle-down effect. You and the staff set the tone for welcoming. Do they greet new people with energy and enthusiasm? Does the secretary's voice on the phone sound suspicious? Is a locked and secure church building more important to the staff than open doors and a welcome banner? I suggest training your staff on the basics of welcoming. I've known church secretaries who are friendly to long term members who stop by to drop off their pledges, but cold as ice to the homeless man who wants a food coupon. It's essential to give anyone who comes into the church the same warm, open welcome. If your staff can't get on board with that, you either need to get them up to speed or suggest they move on.

Finally, do your staff members take ownership of growth? Do they see growing the church as their responsibility? For example, does your Christian education director understand growth as a key part of her role as she plans for next year's curriculum? Does the church sexton see growth as one reason he keeps the place clean?

And I don't need to remind you of this fact: only a growing church can afford payroll. A dying church reduces its staff. Therefore, the fundamentals of growing a church should be incorporated into everything your church staff does, including how they present themselves, how they respond to the needs of the church members, and how they view their job descriptions. You are responsible for training the staff and taking the lead in making church growth a top priority.

The topic of this chapter isn't so much "fire the staff" as it is "Pastor, take charge." That act of "taking charge" includes everyone from the sexton to the kitchen ladies. You are the pastor and your first responsibility is to do

> You are the pastor and your first responsibility is to do what's right for the church. And growing the church is right.

what's right for the church. And growing the church is right. You can be compassionate and appropriate, but there comes a time when you have to replace a person with someone else. It isn't easy, but no one said everything about parish ministry is easy. You can do it.

Peter's Commentary

Yes, you can do it, but speaking from experience as moderator, I don't think you have to do it on your own. Chances are, the staff challenges you see are witnessed and experienced by others as well.

Speaking from experience as a professional salesperson, the issue of how front line employees greet customers and prospective customers is a critical, and often overlooked, dynamic of business development.

Organizations spend millions of dollars to get the prospective customer in-the-door. Yet, if the first point of contact doesn't know how to interact with the prospect, you're in trouble. This engagement doesn't have to be anything over the top and intrusive; but it does need to be welcoming, appreciative, and helpful.

Recently I ventured into one of those large retail electronics megastores to purchase a new laptop computer. I expected this to be a straightforward transaction, because I'd done research and selected three models I wanted to see before making a final decision. I felt comfortable with the approach of checking them out, choosing one, and buying it.

My debit card was warmed-up and ready to be swiped. In others words I was a motivated prospect ready to buy. The investment the company made in advertising on television and bombarding my mail box with fliers had done its job. Now all they had to do was get the product into my hands and remove the cash from my debit account.

Enter the electronics megastore sales professional.

I approached the computer section with their multiple samples on display and started to browse for the brand and models I had pre-selected. Just as I located the first sample, a sales person approached. He was well dressed in the electronics megastore standard issue uniform and struck a kind, helpful demeanor as he asked if he could help me.

I told him exactly what I needed.

He responded to my answer with a huge yawn that reminded me of my 17-year-old cat waking from long nap. I didn't think much about it as anyone can have a rough night and perhaps he was just starting his shift.

This first yawn occurred at the 20 second mark of our selling interaction.

The second yawn occurred 20 seconds later. To be fair, it was less pronounced than the first yawn, but still noticeable enough to interrupt the flow of marketing comments he bombarded me with. In fact, the yawning rendered his words undecipherable, and weakened the likelihood that this "done-deal" transaction was going to happen. I know I'm not boring enough to be yawned at twice in 40 seconds. The fact that his company invested millions of dollars to get prospects into their stores, and I was a live customer, ready to buy, should have energized him. It did not.

Here's where the rubber hits the road: the sales person brings all that investment to life with a closed deal.

The third and final yawn occurred at the 65 second mark. Just as in baseball where three strikes means you're out—this electronics megastore sales professional had struck out. I was now completely uninterested in completing a transaction at this time, in this store, with this salesman.

"That's it. I'm done!" I said to the guy. I walked out of the store. I don't believe he tried to stop me. I think he was too tired to give it a fight.

Sitting in my car, I reflected on the irony of the significant investment the company made to get me in there, but a sales professional who couldn't act in a professional manner became the weak link in the chain; a link that snapped under pressure and lost the deal.

I headed to the next store—the largest competitor of the yawner's company. There, I met an alert sales professional eager to help me view the models I had pre-selected. After we discussed the computers, he advised me to wait five days because new models were coming in the following Saturday and the new version of my first choice was the best buy for me—and part of the software I needed would be included at no charge.

Five days later, I returned.

Peter, the sales rep was there, and while another sales associate was available and asked if he could assist me, I said I'd wait for Peter—who was helping a couple select a television. Once he was finished serving them, Peter turned to me.

"Do you remember me from earlier this week?" I asked.

He responded. "Yes, I do. Let me show the two models you may be interested in."

Forty minutes later I left the store with a new laptop, feeling satisfied with all aspects of the buying experience, including Peter's approach to closing the deal.

Ironically his store wasn't the first one I thought of when I made the decision to buy. From now on, it will be my first and only choice.

My experience, repeated hundreds of time, can set the flywheel of success or failure in motion. Are you, and your staff (paid and unpaid) prepared to properly represent your church?

Making it Happen Worksheet

Pastor, take charge! As the pastor your first responsibility is to do what's right for the church. And growing the church is right. You can be compassionate and appropriate, but there comes a time when you have to replace a person. We know this isn't easy, and the following ideas should help:

Do you have job descriptions for your staff?

_____

Do you hold regular meetings with staff or committee chairs where they can give voice to their concerns and you can find out how they are feeling?

_____

List four ways you could acknowledge and reward great performances.

1. _____

2. _____

3. _____

4. _____

List four ways you could address/mentor performance deficiencies.

1. _____

2. _____

3. _____

4. _____

List four steps to begin the process of discontinuing a staff member's employment.

1. _____

2. _____

3. _____

4. _____

How is that process communicated to the board and lay leadership?

_____

_____

Do you have four tangible reasons for making the change? Include how this will directly benefit the church.

1. _____

2. _____

3. _____

4. _____

If appropriate to do so, how is the decision and action
communicated to the congregation?

_____

_____

Chapter Seven

A Good Sermon is Everything

By Peter

The Bad Sermon

Seated in the third row of pews, I noticed the glassy eyes of the woman to my right. A man on my left pushed up his sleeve to check his watch. With a gentle sigh he pushed the shirt cuff back to its original position. Most of the choir appeared to be daydreaming. In fact, I'm sure a couple of them were actually asleep. I felt compelled to turn around and check the time on the antique clock at the back of the sanctuary. How much longer could this go on?

As I turned to glance at the clock, I saw boredom, confusion, and active dislike mirrored in other faces. I wasn't the only one led into the weeds by the pastor's sermon, and my patience was gone.

The Good Sermon

The sermon ended too soon. I checked my watch, surprised to see twenty minutes had breezed past. I was literally on the edge of my seat, leaning closer so I wouldn't miss a single nuance of meaning or application to everyday life. The words carried a powerful message, enhanced by a delivery that was assertive, rhythmic, deliberately paced, and occasionally slow to add emphasis. Moments of silence punctuated the message. From my balcony seat I could see the pastor occasionally glance at his typed sermon, gracefully turning pages with no delay in presentation—as though he had memorized the sermon, yet wanted to be sure he was staying true to what he'd written. This was artful, for he maintained almost constant eye contact with the congregation. His eyes moved from left-to-right, down to his notes, and then back up to the congregation—to a different person each time. The dance continued, never distracting from the power of the words, but always engaging with someone in the congregation. This was delivering a message at its best. It was a performance.

I knew his words would resonate with me long after I returned home after visiting this Connecticut church. What an inspiration!

I waited to greet the pastor until the receiving line had almost wound down. My conversation with him needed to be more than the standard perfunctory greeting. After fifteen minutes, it was my turn and I made my introduction.

Speaking from the heart, I conveyed to the pastor how compelling his sermon had been, and how moved I was by its message.

Upon my request, he printed a copy of the sermon for me. The document was quite impressive; fourteen pages; double spaced type in a large font. Each page was numbered and had one or two handwritten edits between the typed lines. He told me he was making final edits right up to the last moment.

I appreciated having a unique view of how he prepared and executed his craft. In my profession I'm often required to give presentations, sometimes to only one person, more often to small groups, and occasionally to larger crowds of 200 or more.

But even my experience wouldn't prepare me for having to write and present a sermon every single week. I see it as a daunting task—an exercise fraught with deadline pressure, rewriting, interruptions, and then to cap it all off, execution.

And what of the churches? The sermon putting people to sleep was given at a church that suffered a downward spiral of reduced attendance, financial contributions, and waning energy.

The life-changing sermon was delivered at a thriving church with standing room only. In fact, police were directing traffic so parishioners could leave the area after the first service and make room for people arriving for the second service.

I understand that a sermon doesn't have to be life changing every time, but it does need to be your showcase, the main event, the fodder for what we'll think about during the week. The good news is, you don't need to memorize your sermons. You don't need to leave the pulpit, wave your arms, and pace back and forth to show how impressive you are. No, we want you to inspire and move us by conveying a heartfelt message. The results of doing that are incredible. I saw it in that successful church in Connecticut, and I've seen Reverend Jane do it on numerous occasions at our church in Grafton. Both churches are growing.

It is magic.

Jane's Commentary

On Sunday morning, I sometimes think people feel a sense of dread at the thought of sitting through a sermon. And I wonder, is that one reason they stay home? My theory is, preach powerfully or at least in an interesting manner, and you have a shot at a faithful and flourishing congregation. Do it badly and even your most devoted people will slowly fade away.

The sermon is indeed your chance to sell. So don't take it lightly. Not by being unprepared. Not by leaving it until five o'clock on Sunday morning. Not by convincing yourself your sermons aren't that important. Perhaps it sounds crass to categorize the Word of God as a selling moment. If it makes you more comfortable, use the word *evangelize* instead of the word *sale.* The sermon is your biggest and best moment to say, "This is me. This is who I am. This is what I will offer you every Sunday if you come to this church."

> Perhaps it sounds crass to categorize the Word of God as a selling moment. If it makes you more comfortable, use the word *evangelize* instead of the word *sale.*

Yet, I am the first to admit—it isn't easy. Last week was a good example. I had the best of intentions. I set aside three blocks of time to write: Tuesday morning, then Thursday almost all day, and then part of Friday. With a feeling of optimism, I sat down at my desk on Tuesday morning and after reading the text through only once, my secretary asked me to work on a project with her—which I needed to do.

Then came a call from a church deacon who asked if I knew one of our elderly church members was having "a terrible time of it and could I visit?" I left my desk immediately and went to the nursing home, sat with the elderly woman and then had a follow up conversation with her daughter, an exhausted caretaker. I returned to my desk just in time to leave for a meeting. But I was still in good shape as I had set aside *all day* Thursday for the sermon. But Thursday morning quickly filled with three different people stopping by the church to talk, an impromptu but necessary meeting with the moderator, and long conversation on the phone with a church member facing the news of a serious medical diagnosis. I left for lunch.

When I got back to my desk I made a stab at the sermon, but honestly, I didn't have much left in me. Although I accomplished a little, it was far from finished. That left almost an entire sermon to finish on Friday. It didn't happen. I had started early, made some progress, but quickly got involved in preparations for the upcoming annual meeting and a few other odds and ends for Sunday worship. Before I knew it, I faced Saturday morning with no sermon. I managed to finish (having absolutely no choice helped) and the sermon seemed good—solid, if not "from the mountaintop". But, I admit, my process wasn't ideal.

I still absolutely agree the sermon has to be good. Not just good but engaging, well-written, and passionately delivered. And that only happens with time, self-discipline, and practice. I'm not saying it's easy. But you can do it.

Making it Happen Worksheet

As the heartbeat of the service, the sermon is a weekly opportunity to capture the imagination, educate, and inspire your parishioners. The best sermons encourage reflection and introspection, strive for the greater good, and serve as outreach to the congregation and wider community.

Identify three days this week to work on the sermon:

_____

On day one, I would like to accomplish....

_____

_____

_____

On day two, I would like to accomplish....

_____

_____

_____

On day three, I would like to accomplish....

_____

_____

_____

When the sermon is prepared, but before the delivery, answer these questions:

What is my favorite part of this sermon?

_____

_____

Where do I get bored?

_____

_____

What is the "take-home" message?

_____

_____

Is an illustration needed?

_____

Where?

_____

How about another one?

_____

Write your concluding sentence. Make it the most important
sentence in the sermon.

_____

_____

Now it's time to practice. Get up in the pulpit while no one's
around and work through your sermon with a friend listening.
Continue to tweak and edit during this time. If you are not in
the habit of practicing your sermon, you'll be surprised by how
it improves with even one entire run-through from the pulpit.

Chapter Eight
Theology is Good, Coffee is Better

By Jane

I stood in the reception line following the worship service when a woman approached me, her hand already extended to shake mine, and a smile on her face. She and her husband had seemed engaged and interested throughout the entire sermon, and since this was only my third Sunday at my new church, all my senses were on overdrive. Every pastor loves praise following a sermon and I am not an exception. Without realizing it, I was happily anticipating a compliment, and here it came. "Pastor," she said, beaming. "I loved your sermon!"

"Well, thank you," I replied trying to look pastoral and not overconfident. "It was fun to do." Fun to do? Where did that come from? I doubt Reinhold Niebuhr ever called his sermons "fun to do."

"Our last pastor was so smart and intellectual, we could hardly understand a thing he said in the pulpit. But not you! You're easy to understand!"

I've heard that before. The last pastor was super smart, but thank goodness I didn't have that problem. Other than saying

I'm not the brightest bulb in the church chandelier, I think people are really saying, "Theology is good, but other things are more important." Or more specifically, "Theology is good, but being in relationship is better." And the sermon is an experience of relationship.

Of course, bringing the Word of God to parishioners with intellectually stimulating sermons that contain challenging ideas and revealing scriptural insight is essential to being a good pastor and growing your church. But if it stops there, then the effort is wasted. Isolated intellect—even in the most urbane congregations—begins to work against you. Developing and maintaining relationship grows a church. In churches where there is no relationship with the pastor, there will be no growth.

Is there such a thing as too smart? A good sermon as well as Bible studies, adult Sunday school, workshops, and small groups should be thought-provoking and challenging. In fact, pastors need to make it a regular practice to leave church members with reasons to think and question. But intellectual moments in the church should also inspire, amuse, and motivate. And although developing one's understanding is imperative to personal development, the overall growth and health of the congregation also depends on your ability to lead the congregation to new places in terms of biblical studies and understanding the nature of God, Jesus, and the Holy Spirit.

But if too smart means no one can listen to you for more than ten minutes without drifting off, or if too smart means you, as pastor, are hiding behind your intellect to avoid the messiness and work of relationship building, then you are, indeed too smart. Establishing relationship with each parishioner is critical

> Developing and maintaining relationship grows a church. In churches where there is no relationship with the pastor, there will be no growth.

to our effectiveness as pastors, and therefore, greatly determines our success or failure in growing a church.

A popular theory among church growth experts is that you cannot establish relationship with each person, but rather you need to farm out the relationship-building to an active church staff. I recently read an article by Rick Warren, popular mega-church pastor that said if you want your church to grow beyond the 120 member mark, the pastor needs to stop doing all the pastoral care herself. You must hand it over to others and focus on delegation and administration. Of course there's some truth to that idea and if your church is over 500 members, I would agree. But most mainline protestant churches are struggling to reach 500. I believe you can get to these higher numbers by establishing relationship with each person and maintaining it— not by delegating relationship-building to others.

People want to be personally connected to the pastor. So let them. Make *relationship* a priority and you will be amazed at how much it will grow your church. As the sales motto goes "I don't care how much you know, I

> People want to be personally connected to the pastor. So let them. Make *relationship* a priority and you will be amazed at how much it will grow your church.

want to know how much you care." The pastor must always be emotionally connected to her parishioners.

What does that mean? First, it means a lot of work. Because keeping up with each person seems almost impossible in our world today. You constantly make an effort to stay aware of your parishioners' needs. So listen during meetings, coffee hour, and youth group. Who is in need of a call, an email, a thank you note, or a quick text? Who in your congregation should you make a special effort to reach? I keep an ongoing list on my smartphone which I can update and turn to every day. And then I meet with my church administrator weekly to review the list. Staying aware and engaged in the lives of your parishioners is critical to maintaining and developing relationship. And it leads to church growth.

Although keeping up with those already in your church is important, engaging directly with visitors is equally crucial. How does one do that on a busy Sunday morning? This is when you need to enlist a team of people who are deliberately trained to get names, greet new people, and talk.

Coffee hour was in full swing when I joined the group following service. I quickly scanned the room as I picked up my cup of coffee. I didn't see the new family who'd slipped into a back pew after the service started. I was particularly interested because this family had seven children, all of whom came forward for the children's sermon. Every table in the fellowship hall was full of church members in groups, talking and laughing. I concluded the new family had decided not to stay for coffee hour. But then I spotted them—sitting alone with no church members even near them. I saw the mother glance around and by the time I quickly made my way across the room to them, she was gathering up coats and sweaters, preparing to leave.

Engaging long term members in the process of welcome is harder than it sounds. For some reason, most church members need lots of encouragement to engage with visitors. In each of my churches, I've started a Welcoming Committee where we deliberately discuss how to welcome, why we do it, and explore the hesitation people

> Engaging long term members in the process of welcome is harder than it sounds.

seem to have. It helps. No more tables of new members isolated from tables of old members.

And remember, although you want to be friendly, don't let the congregation "swarm" new people. Unfortunately some of our churches are so desperate for new members, especially young people, that when someone does visit, the new person is mobbed—and you may never see them again. Train your people to be purposeful greeters who use discretion. In other words, they know how much is too much. Additionally, when a new person shows interest, you can't immediately load them up with church jobs. Just because a family has young children doesn't mean the mother wants to join Board of Christian Education. Or just because your new member is a contractor doesn't mean he or she wants to chair the Buildings and Grounds Committee. Let new members find their way. Some will jump in with both feet, while others engage more slowly.

The most effective outreach I've done as a pastor is to invite small groups of regular visitors to my house for an evening I call Prospective Member Fellowship. I invite anyone who has been coming to church for a few weeks, as well as several long term members who have positive things to say about the church. The evening, which takes place about every two months, has grown my churches more than anything else I've ever done.

As new and old members gather at my house (I serve wine and good food, by the way), we sit around the living room in a circle just talking. Eventually I call us to order and ask each person to tell their story, especially what brought them to the church. This includes the old members. Hearing each person's story is interesting and sometimes emotional. From old members, I often learn things I hadn't known and maybe would never have learned if they hadn't come to my house for this event. From the new or prospective members, I gain insight into what brought them to our church.

The evening progresses and at the end of it, I ask, point blank, "Who wants to join the church this Sunday?" The response is almost always very positive. That evening is their entire "orientation" to church membership.

I've been criticized for not offering new member classes. Most mainline churches require a class on what it means to be a member of their particular church and denomination. I don't. I think the most importation piece of joining a church is *relationship*. The rest will come later. And anyway, who wants to join a church only be handed a thick three-ring binder and told to attend a class?

Finally, once people have joined, as pastor you have to make sure you don't drop them like hot potatoes. I had a thriving fellowship group once for all the people who joined the church within the past year. They met for social events, sat together in church, and became a support system for each other. But then it fell apart. The woman who organized the group and kept it going decided it was too much for her (a reasonable issue) and dropped out of the leadership role. No one stepped up. So I tried to lead the group. And I failed. The new members stayed with the church, but occasionally one would wistfully ask if someone could take over the group again. In retrospect, could I have done something better? Yes. Instead of stepping in, I should have empowered a new leader. I didn't. Remember, when it comes to new members, relationship is everything. And not just with the pastor.

Theology is good, coffee is better.

> I think the most importation piece of joining a church is *relationship*. The rest will come later.

Peter's Commentary

I've come to know Reverend Jane over the past few months. First, from the thorough review of her candidate profile, then by pouring through her supplemental materials: video-taped sermons, photographs, other writings, and her excellent references. Next came the interview process with the excitement and energy of reaching agreement on a contract for her to join our church. And then her weekly sermons (fantastic), her outreach efforts to the community (outstanding), her engagement with every committee in the church (unbelievable), and finally our collaboration on this project.

So, I completely agree with her: Theology is Good, Coffee is Better. Reverend Jane lives this credo, and it's a rare occasion when a meeting doesn't include, either directly or indirectly, something to do with coffee. The single serve coffee maker now adorning her office gets a lot of use, for just as the famous coffee houses create an exceptional environment to enjoy coffee and conversation, so does Jane's office.

Speaking of coffee, Jane's decision to change where coffee is served during our post-service coffee hour dramatically affected two elements of the coffee hour experience each week. First, more people attend. And secondly, they stay longer and the energy and buzz in the vestry is infectious.

Where did she move the coffee serving area?

She moved it from the kitchen counters on the far side of the vestry to smack-dab in the middle of the vestry. Now people surround the coffee serving area, gently moving in to get their coffee and then moving out to allow others access to the coffee urns. This simple physical change had a dramatic effect.

Think about how you can create the ultimate coffee-and-fellowship experience in your church. A simple move may be all you need.

Chapter Nine

The Forever Search

By Peter

Last October, a friend at a church in New Hampshire told me they were expecting their search for a new pastor to take two years. A member of a nearby central Massachusetts church told me her search committee had been meeting every Wednesday night for two-and-a-half years; and finally, the upstate New York church told me last December that their search process had been going on for three years with no end in sight.

Why?

Having experienced the wonderful end result of being on a search committee and finding the right pastor—and everything that goes along with it—I should be content because the process worked as advertised and the committee's long hours of meetings and independent review and reflection all bore fruit. I should be satisfied and happy. Well, I'm not.

Am I satisfied with the outcome? Yes, absolutely. Am I content? Not quite. I am absolutely convinced the process doesn't need to take eighteen to thirty-six months, or even more.

Despite how wonderful an interim pastor may be, (and I think we were lucky in our church to have one of the best interims) the longer the period of time in transition, the more challenging it is to grow the church. I think any opportunity to compress the search process is a critical component in stabilizing a dormant or failing church and reversing its course. Perhaps we've reached the point where the process requires a second look and can be streamlined to make it more efficient.

From personal experience and after discussing the search process with three other searching churches and two synagogues, I see specific areas where the cycle could be compressed. I understand some churches don't want to change any element of what they're doing. This chapter is not for them.

However, if you see merit in a more efficient process that produces the same outcome as the long, drawn out, somewhat antiquated process—then here you go. I see this as a ten-step progression: each step containing defined timelines and objectives. One of the ten steps includes waiting for information and input, but if handled properly that won't interrupt the flow.

Nominating process: Gather a diverse group of members across a broad spectrum of characteristics: Long-tenured members, newer members, male, female, older members, and younger members. Move deliberately through the nominating process and clearly explain what it means to join the committee.

Meeting frequency and objectives: Select a committee chairperson. This person should bring to the position a proven ability, either in a church-based group or secular group (business, community, or school) to handle group dynamics. Define a meeting schedule, timing of meetings, and objectives and responsibilities. Also define voting protocols. For example, does the group need to vote unanimously in favor of proceeding with a candidate, or is a simple majority required? Similarly, is a unanimous vote to make a call recommendation to the congregation required for the selected candidate, or does a majority vote suffice? It is absolutely crucial to establish these parameters at the beginning as they will most certainly come into play later, when issues will be harder to reconcile.

Write your church profile: This means a focus on the three key elements to attracting the candidates you want. Jump starting your church means you're able to sell your church in a forty word overview. That may be a challenge when your church is 250 years old, but this vital description will either attract prospective candidates to you or drive them away to look elsewhere. Your entire profile may end up being forty pages long, but that forty-word description for the employment opportunity will trigger the engagement of the strong candidate.

Reviewing candidate profiles: Read the profiles, but don't take too much time analyzing every element. Get to the sermon! Yes, reviewing profiles needs to be a thoughtful, prayerful process, yet I'll use a baseball analogy to describe what I think is the most important element of considering a candidate BEFORE you actually make the decision to interview.

Whether it's little league tryouts, middle school, high school, or college tryouts, when a player indicates an interest in pitching, what's the one thing he or she must show the coach? That's right—the player has to actually THROW THE BALL. That one action says it all.

In our search process, I believe we spent too much time examining every element of a candidate's background and capabilities before we decided to hear a sermon. After all, isn't that where the rubber meets the road? Can he or she deliver a great sermon? Does the delivery show a strong ability to inspire, teach, and lead? If the answer is no, then what else matters? A good sermon is everything!

Think of how much time a search committee can save by moving to this step sooner. I sat in many a search committee meeting where, after lengthy and spirited discussion about how a candidate looked on paper, we finally decided to view a sermon on video. Every time, within minutes of watching a candidate in action, each committee member was able to reach a decision.

The lesson is—if you have even a cursory interest in a candidate, once you see a sermon you'll be amazed at how quickly you can reach a decision to move forward or disengage.

The interview process: Step 1: Initial candidate interviews. The most important part of this phase is how your committee prepares for the interview. Formulate your questions in advance and decide ahead of time who will ask them. Also decide who will answer the candidate's questions about key areas of your church, such as

♦ Leadership

♦ Missions

♦ Christian education

♦ Finances

♦ Capital projects

♦ Deacons

♦ Music

♦ Children

♦ Community

♦ Open-and-Affirming

♦ Pledging

♦ How you talk about "money"

Decide what process you'll follow after the interview. For example, will the committee meet directly afterward to discuss the candidate? Or, do you elect to do that the next day, or two days later so people can reflect on the experience? What is the process for voting on whether to continue the candidacy and hearing everyone's opinion on the candidate? (In my opinion if you come out of an initial interview with anything less than a consensus on positive energy and momentum, you probably don't have a candidate who's going to win over the congregation.)

Step two is the all-important second interview. This is the big one! What did you miss in the first interview? What are the areas of concern? What will you tell the congregation—should it reach that stage—about why you like this particular candidate? During this meeting you should be prepared for more focused questions from the candidate, such as

+ Why would I want to lead this congregation?

+ Would I be able to work with them?

+ How will decision making be handled?

+ What's the parsonage like?

+ What's the community like?

+ Do you truly want to grow your church?

+ Do members seem to embrace change or fight it?

Checking references: I've worked in the employment staffing and placement industry for many years, and my best advice for you is to take references with the proverbial grain of salt. Look for gaps in employment history. Do a background check, and make sure you ask candidates about the circumstances of why they are leaving, or have left, prior positions.

In my opinion, the unique perspectives of your nine-member search committee who ask the right questions should have much more weight than references in telling you how great a particular candidate may be.

When you find the one: Stop the process! You've done it! You selected a candidate, made the offer, and received an acceptance. You're done.

Well, not quite.

The search committee toiled for months and months, and in some cases, years. The finish line is now in sight and the anticipation of this great candidate taking over is intoxicating. But you're only halfway there, because the congregation that entrusted you to complete this process *hasn't met your candidate.*

Be prepared with a thorough description of both the candidate and why you think that person is right for your church at this time. A compelling, spirited, heartfelt overview for the congregation is an absolute requirement. Furthermore, how, and by whom, this message goes out is another critical component.

Candidate Sunday: Showtime! Again, preparation for this all-important juncture in the process is critical. How has the committee prepared the congregation for this moment? For example, has a Meet-the-Candidate dinner been convened? Have you given other committee chairs an opportunity to talk with the new pastor before candidate Sunday? How are you helping the candidate prepare for the occasion? This will be a stressful occasion for the candidate and his or her family.

Make sure that when your candidate goes up to the pulpit to deliver the sermon, it isn't the first time he or she has been there. And don't forget the elements of lighting and sound, so your pastor can be heard and seen, literally in the best light.

Congregational vote, then get going: The sermon has been delivered, the service has come to a close, the candidate leaves the sanctuary, and the moderator leads a special congregational meeting to vote on the pastor. I recommend the search committee members stand in front of the congregation, ready to answer questions during the discussion period.

After the vote is taken—likely in the affirmative if you've done all your homework—a new era in the history of your church will begin.

Well done, search committee! Now you're finished!

Jane's Commentary

For once, Peter and I are in complete agreement. A prolonged search process forces churches into a kind of death-by-waiting. By the time the new pastor is finally called to the church, the congregation has limped along for nearly two years, sometimes longer. This lack of leadership (a few interims are very effective and actually grow the church, but many are ineffective and do not seem concerned with growth) will leave a struggling church in the throes of near death, or a previously thriving church facing decline.

I agree that following the ten steps Peter delineates could dramatically reduce the search process, in some cases to as little as six months. Again, for churches in transition this means you're closer to initiating that new chapter in the church's history.

Why is it like this? The endless search and call process is from another era—an era before Skype, Web-ex, and the Cloud. If we can now gain access to profiles, sermon videos, and personal blogs at the click of a keyboard, why do we still have timelines that reflect hardcopies and waiting on the mail? If we now have the ability to Web-ex, why do we wait for the night everyone can "get together" to meet? Like everything, the church is often the last to jump on board. When it comes to Search and Call, we are far behind.

> The endless search and call process is from another era—an era before Skype, Web-ex, and the Cloud.

But it isn't only the appropriate use of electronics that should streamline the process. The real reason to move ahead at a more efficient speed is the fact that our world doesn't wait for anyone anymore. When I was doing search and call as a pastor, I sent my profile out to 10 or 15 search committees. Within three months, I had a call that I accepted. Two months after working at my new church, I received a letter from one of the churches to whom I sent my profile.

"We are prayerfully and carefully considering your profile and are very excited about your qualifications. We will be contacting you in the near future." Too late. Why did that search committee take five months to respond to my profile? And when I contacted them to say I'd taken another position, they seemed genuinely surprised and disappointed.

Our antiquated system is too long, and it hurts both pastors and churches. Time to enter the 21st Century!

Making it Happen Worksheet

Detail the elements of your ten step process from commencement of the search process to a successful acceptance of your call (offer of employment).

1. Selection process for the Search and Call Committee

_____

_____

_____

2. Meeting frequency and objectives

_____

_____

_____

3. Writing your church profile: timing, authors, and review process

_____

_____

_____

4. Reviewing candidate profiles: What will our process be?

_____

_____

_____

5. Step one of the two step interview process—procedures, rules of engagement, and outcome objectives

_____

_____

_____

6. Step two of the two step interview process – procedures, rules of engagement, and outcome objectives

_____

_____

_____

7. Checking references

_____

_____

_____

8. Call recommendation process

_____

_____

_____

9. Candidate Sunday: Showtime!

_____

_____

_____

10. Congregational vote

_____

_____

_____

Chapter Ten

What Does Your Church Offer that Youth Soccer Doesn't?

By Jane

"No one comes to church anymore, because they're all at sports." My colleague voiced a complaint I hear all the time from ministers, Christian Education committee chairs, Sunday school teachers, and youth group leaders. You name it—if the person works in the church, they've grown to resent youth sports. Few things are more discouraging to a pastor or youth leader than the dominance of sports in our culture. You want to grow your church, yet your biggest competitor is organized, well-budgeted, and loved by everyone.

Sports feels like the enemy. It isn't.

How does today's pastor compete with the many activities tugging at the small amount of time a family has together? My answer—you don't. We should choose not to compete simply because we don't have to. A church that's doing its job offers something no youth soccer league, baseball team, or dance troupe can provide. The church is an entirely different entity with different goals, clients, and dreams. Don't enter the competition. Instead, commit to being alive and out there in a way the generation of pastors before you didn't even consider.

So the question is—how? How do you grow your church in a way that honors families who gain so much from sports events, and yet demonstrates to the world there is more to life than having your kid make the traveling baseball team? Pastors need to approach the sports issue proactively—if their goal really is to grow their church.

First, you need to learn to co-exist. Soccer and baseball are not going away. We will never go back to the days when Wednesday night was church night. In fact, we will never go back to the days when Sunday morning was reserved for church. As discouraging as that is, the best thing you can do as a pastor is get over it. Those days are over and maybe that's a good thing. It makes our job harder, but at least people are not going to church by default. Think of this as an opportunity instead of bemoaning the fact that things aren't what they used to be.

What do I mean by learning to co-exist? I mean that instead of fighting against the hectic schedule of today's parents and church members, figure out how to work with it. I have sat through countless clergy meetings as my colleagues complained bitterly because everyone was attending the Boy Scout Jamboree this weekend instead of church. As clergy, we need to recognize how important these moments are for our families, and then accommodate their schedules.

We do everyone a disservice—including ourselves—by digging in our heels and insisting that confirmation is only valid if kids and parents keep to a rigid schedule; or that the youth group must stay with its traditional time of Sunday night at 6:30. Face it, youth sports are going to win when it comes to family priorities. Live with it. Organize your church events so families can do both, and graciously accept it when baseball wins over church. The thing about sports is that if kids don't attend, they often don't get to play. Offer a church experience that celebrates when the kid is there and offers no guilt or pressure when she's playing shortstop.

Most importantly, you can't take it personally when a family chooses sports over you. It isn't you. It's the circumstance of our time. You will do a lot more to "sell your church" if it's a guilt free, happy place than a place where the pastor makes kids and parents feel bad about missing.

Second, use sports events as an opportunity to grow your church. That may sound counterintuitive, but it isn't. You've heard the phrase, "if you can't beat 'em, join 'em?"

> Most importantly, you can't take it personally when a family chooses sports over you. It isn't you. It's the circumstance of our time.

This is a great time to put that concept into practice.

Here's how. My last church was in Iowa, and in Iowa—especially the small towns—baseball is king. The baseball schedule is exhaustingly rigorous—especially for families with more than one child. I know parents who spend every night, six or seven days a week during June and July, on the baseball field. They work all day, rush home, make a quick dinner, and take everyone to the game. They get the kids into their uniforms, find ball gloves and cleats, and deal with melt-downs, all the while ignoring their own fatigue in the desperate goal of getting everyone to the game. These are people who need your support as pastor more than ever. They certainly don't need our frustration that they don't give the same amount of energy to church.

One summer, I decided to attend one game for every church child. I asked each family to give me the baseball or softball schedule for their child/children. When they heard I wanted to attend a game of their offspring, their excitement and gratitude were surprising. In other words, they were thrilled. I then entered one game per kid into my calendar and spent the month of June sitting in the stands in various parks and recreation centers all over town. If your church is small to medium sized, you can do this with a little planning. In this particular church only one child wasn't involved in baseball, so I attended his piano recital.

I started it as an experiment (and I have to admit, a little begrudgingly—I'm not a big sports fan). But to my surprise, the experience was extraordinary. It proved a great opportunity to connect with the parents and grandparents of each child or youth and to show that I was truly interested. I sat in the stands with the families, cheered on the kids and listened as parents and grandparents spoke about their lives. They told me all kinds of things they probably wouldn't have shared in another setting— certainly not in the church building or at a church event. These evenings on the baseball field exponentially strengthened my relationship with each family—through all generations. I ended up with families who knew I cared about what was important to them and to their children. The pay-off was big.

Peter's Commentary

Okay, reality-check time.

For a seven-year period after Mary and I joined the church, I conveniently "scheduled" Sunday mornings as one of my critical exercise periods for the week. I convinced myself that because I had to don a suit-and-tie Monday thru Friday for work, I was excused from that on Sunday mornings. While Sunday mornings were absolutely church time for Mary and our daughters, it was my time to do whatever I wanted, which most of the time meant exercising in one way or another. I was even "excused" from church by the (then) assistant pastor who justified my decision-making to Mary, explaining something to the effect that if it was my time "for reflection," then it was okay. I wonder what she was really thinking!

Fast forward to 2014, and hopefully a more mature approach based upon the premise, and the realization, that I have plenty of other opportunities to exercise during the week, and Sunday morning doesn't need to be one of them. Yes, I believe that goes for team events too, and kudos to parents who can engage with sports coaches in a thoughtful discussion of this subject.

Pastor Jane makes a good point, but I disagree with her on this. I think she's too accommodating; and so was the former associate pastor. I wish she'd helped me by holding me to a higher standard. We need to raise the bar. We're in a culture where everyone gets a trophy, after all.

To show true leadership, a pastor needs the self-confidence to say that church should be a priority for everyone.

Get a life and leave Sunday mornings open. You can find other times to workout, exercise, or sleep. We only get one Sunday morning per week, and your kids will learn a lifelong lesson when they see you placing church above worldly things.

Making it Happen Worksheet

1. Ask each parent or grandparent in your church for a baseball or softball schedule. The best time to do this is during the last two weeks of May.

2. Look at the schedules and then enter one game per child on your calendar.

3. Start attending games! Usually, all baseball and softball is over by the end of June.

4. If you have church kids who are not in sports, ask what they're interested in. See if you can attend a piano recital, choir concert, or a play.

Before the game: list three ways your church can help these athletes on the field.

1. _____

2. _____

3. _____

Chapter Eleven
If You Don't Feel Dynamic—Fake it!

By Peter

After working with hundreds of other sales professionals, I'm convinced a direct connection exists between success and being dynamic and engaging with clients.

I believe the same holds true for pastors.

The most successful pastors are able to exude energy and vitality. No, the pastor doesn't need to be "on" all the time like an animated machine, but these traits are essential in certain critical areas. The purpose of this chapter is to discuss three of those areas.

When it comes to church growth, a dynamic pastor is the greatest asset a church can have. A dynamic attitude enhances her ability to lead, motivate, and inspire her congregation in many ways. From my perspective as a member of the congregation and moderator, I think the three critical times for dynamic behavior are as follows:

1. The sermon

2. The short period of time before the worship service as people are arriving

3. Coffee hour

The sermon: A friend recently called me to talk about a new interim minister at her church in New York. She explained the minister had arrived at the church with many accolades, based on her credentials. There was significant excitement in the congregation in anticipation of her first sermon.

But there was a problem, my friend said.

"The minister is boring." My friend went on to tell me about the sermons. Her account was fascinating, and I especially noticed how she sequenced her comments, which told me what mattered the most to her.

It sounded as though this minister did the perfunctory things well. Her sermons started with six minutes of reciting scripture, then occasionally a quick joke. But the body of the sermon was too repetitive.

"It seems like she's losing her place." My friend said. "Or, maybe she's making it up as she goes along. She repeats herself over and over; it's like she forgets to study the night before." My friend was disappointed after feeling such high hopes for this pastor. The minister wasn't dynamic.

> When you aren't fully prepared for a sermon and make things up as you go along, it's challenging to be truly dynamic.

When you aren't fully prepared for a sermon and make things up as you go along, it's challenging to be truly dynamic.

Not a great way to provide ministry—interim, or otherwise.

What is the potential impact to a church's growth trajectory? Granted, it could be minimal if this pastor delivers better presentations on upcoming Sundays. But, what if she doesn't?

The other two critical areas are the few minutes before the start of the worship service and the coffee hour.

Welcoming prior to the worship service: I realize greeting people before the service begins can be a challenge because of timing and responsibilities. But when a pastor can pull it off, the benefits are tremendous. Are you able to spend a few minutes at the door welcoming members and guests to the service? This is important for connecting with your congregants, and equally vital to connect and introduce yourself to guests and visitors. They will enjoy having this point-of-reference when you introduce the service and deliver your super dynamic sermon.

Coffee hour: This is less challenging from a time commitment as your service will be behind you; but it's a challenge from the perspective of working the room. What do I mean by working the room? I mean reaching out to as many people as possible; engaging with each person in a specific way—being an active listener, and then moving on to the next person or family you want to speak with. The best pastors I've seen have an amazing ability to remember people's names, and can recollect at least one point-of-interest for each member to reference in the conversation. You may want to prepare for sitting down with the parishioners who are seated during coffee hour. This mirroring approach reflects how much you care and want to connect with them.

If you nailed the working-the-room issue associated with coffee hour, you'll probably be exhausted when the final hour comes to an end.

But the return for your dynamic welcome, a dynamic sermon, and your dynamic presence at coffee hour means this three hour period of time on Sunday morning/early afternoon can set a positive trajectory for the entire week.

One could argue that the pastor should always be "on" and ready. I recall a minister saying he was told by a parishioner on a Monday, "I saw you in the hardware store on Saturday, and you didn't look very happy!" That's a bit much.

But I do think the pastor in a growing church has a responsibility to build constituencies, alliances, and relationships wherever he or she may be. Most importantly, that should begin with a great worship service that includes a memorable sermon, bookended by the opportunity to be engaging and dynamic in the few minutes leading up to the service and the sixty minutes following the service during coffee hour.

Jane's Commentary

Easy for Peter to say. His observation that a pastor should be "engaging and dynamic" before, during, and after the service is a lot harder than he—or any parishioner—realizes. And yet, it is the absolute truth. A pastor needs to make total use of these valuable minutes to connect with the people in the church. There will be people who may never come back if they don't feel appropriately welcomed in the time before the service. During coffee hour, I see people who look awkward standing around with coffee cups and no one, especially the pastor, to talk with them.

Here's the difficult piece. The entire church needs/wants some of the pastor's time before the service and during coffee hour. So the pastor isn't just there to greet new people—but really, to greet everyone. So how do you handle this, since visitors more than anyone need special attention? There are two options—and I found that employing both is helpful. One is to train a welcoming staff who will spot newcomers and make sure they're greeted. Another is to have a competent group of church members—in my case, the diaconate—who take on setting up and running the worship service, freeing you to welcome.

The time at home following the Sunday service is my most exhausted, yet peaceful, time of the week. In fact, I love Sunday afternoons. Not because I am glad the service is over (a small part of me is of *course* glad it's over) but because this is the calm after the storm. And in my case, a good storm. Sunday morning is a storm of emotion, interaction, relationship renewal, and always—welcoming. And it's a storm I plunge into with all my energy and as Peter would say "engagement." But it is difficult. Sunday is certainly a time when the pastor must be "all things to all people."

Making it Happen Worksheet

Here are some practices I've found helpful as a pastor. See if you can incorporate a few:

♦ Identify a welcoming, extroverted church member. Ask him or her to keep an eye out for visitors and welcome them for you. Have your "welcomer" jot down the names of each visitor and give the list to you.

♦ Following coffee hour, make a quick list of any new names. Cross reference with your welcoming person.

Chapter Twelve
Open Your House, Open Your Heart

By Jane

The house was finally ready. Plates of Christmas cookies, finger sandwiches, and rows of wine glasses sat waiting on the long dining room table. Every inch of the small parsonage was decorated for the holidays. A fire burned in the hearth and candles flickered at each window. Even the dog had been groomed and sported a red and green neckerchief. Christmas carols played softly in the background. This was the yearly Christmas Open House when I invited the entire church to come by and have a cup of Christmas cheer.

All was going smoothly until Carol, a long-time member of the church, walked in, glanced into the dining room, and said in a loud voice, "Look at that table! Not a homemade dessert on it. Do you think she's ever baked anything in her life?" She was referring to the fact that I hired a caterer for the party. My church was in a small farming community where cooking and baking were important. It didn't matter how much I planned or paid for this party—in Carol's opinion, it wasn't good enough and she felt perfectly comfortable letting everyone know how she felt. I remember being more angry and disappointed than I wanted to admit.

I believe church growth is more likely to happen if the pastor invites church members into her home. The drawback of course, as seen with Carol, is that letting church members into your life (in this case, your house) can mean they feel free to be open with their opinions of you. After my experience that Christmas, I was less enthusiastic—at least for a while—about church events at my house. I got over it fairly quickly, but it took a little working through on my part.

> I believe church growth is more likely to happen if the pastor invites church members into her home.

Why open your house to the church? Lots of pastors don't do it, but many do. Of course, this partly depends on your spouse or partner. If your family isn't on board, then you should figure out some other way to connect. But if inviting people into your home is a possibility, by all means do it. You'll be surprised at how this single act will increase your ministry and help grow your church.

The evening started slowly with quiet conversation as about fifteen people—new members and old—mingled a little warily. An older woman, Lois, sat in a chair by the window a bit apart from the crowd. I didn't know Lois well—she had been attending services sporadically, and so I invited her to the prospective member's event at my house. She seemed especially taken aback at the young couple with the tattoos and the boisterous seven year old who ran up and down our basement stairs alternately watching the Disney movie I had plugged in and checking on his single dad who was sitting beside the fireplace engaged in serious conversation with our church moderator. The prospective members' gathering was off to a good start. I would keep an eye on Lois—she seemed a little overwhelmed.

I typically host a gathering for anyone who's been attending church but isn't yet a member. The gathering is at my house and happens about every two to three months—whenever I have a group of people who seem like potential members. I also invite long-time members who will be welcoming and who clearly love the church. And I am careful to invite people of all ages and backgrounds. I fill the table with wine and food and let the guests mingle for about an hour. After that, I gather everyone into a circle. Everyone introduces themselves and tells how they came to attend our church. Sometimes the stories are emotional, and sometimes funny. They are always revealing.

These are productive evenings for many reasons. First, I have the chance to know a prospective member in a different way than meeting only at a church service. As an added bonus, I often learn new things about long-term members. I'm always interested to learn how someone ended up at my church. These meetings at my house are great ways for me to evaluate what my church looks and feels like to visitors. I also ask our long-term members to tell us what keeps them coming.

The evening usually ends fairly soon after everyone is done sharing, or when the last bottle of wine is empty. Before everyone leaves, I ask if they want to commit to joining the church that Sunday. I'm always encouraged by how enthusiastic people feel about joining. They might have come to my house not sure how they felt about the church, but they almost always leave ready to jump on board. Or as Peter would say, "You closed the deal."

I don't believe enthusiasm for the church would be as strong if I held the meeting in the church basement. Even if you have a warm and welcoming room in your church, the atmosphere of a pastor's house changes things. A real home turns a membership meeting into an intimate and comfortable party. Being at the pastor's home also makes the gathering more relaxed than sitting on metal folding chairs in the fellowship hall. New people especially need to feel they're in a non-threatening environment. The pastor's home is a safe place for sharing one's faith journey and then starting on a new aspect of that journey.

Lois joined the church that Sunday. She became one of our most committed members and never tired of telling the story of that evening at the pastor's house.

Open your house and open your heart. The reward will be new members and new relationships.

Peter's Commentary

The symbolism of "opening your house" holds true for any occasion. For example, I've attended events in the modest home of an interim pastor during his brief tenure in the parsonage, and this gathering had more warmth and welcome than events at more "regal" settings with all the trappings and accoutrements.

The willingness to bring people into your home is a fundamental step in church growth. Quickly forget about trying to make everyone happy all the time. The overwhelming majority opinion will be warmth and appreciation, creating a strong spirit of "we're all in this together." Just as having a dinner party, brunch, or get-together of any kind in a secular setting can be nerve-racking and angst producing, you'll probably feel stressed when hosting as a pastor. Yet this kind gesture is worth any pressure you may feel, because the memories created during these occasions last a long time.

Open your house, open your heart, and watch your congregation energize and grow.

The wonderful thing about these gathering is they don't need to happen often. Three or four times a year is perfect. Open your house, open your heart, and watch your congregation energize and grow.

Making it Happen Worksheet

If welcoming church people into your home works for both you and your spouse or partner, make plans to get started.

Start small. Invite a struggling committee to have a meeting at your home. A change in atmosphere may be beneficial to the group's energy. On the lines below, identify three committees that could use a boost:

1. _____

2. _____

3. _____

List three people who could bring food:

1. _____

2. _____

3. _____

List two people who could stay to help clean up:

1. _____

2. _____

Chapter Thirteen
The Lights are too Bright, the Music is too Loud

By Peter

The cabinet meeting agenda item was clear. Bullet-pointed on the agenda was the word "Lighting." We had a problem with the lights.

My absolute requirements for the parishioner experience of sitting in church are the following:

- Is the sanctuary warm? Can you feel your fingers and toes on a cold winter day?

- Does the sanctuary have a decent sound-system? Can you hear what's going on?

- Is the sanctuary well-lit? Can you see what's going on?

A trustee at the meeting said "I'll get on that—let me speak to the electrician. I'll see what we can do."

Two weeks later the report of a solution created a spark of energy among the cabinet members. The electrician working with the trustee recommended LED bulbs to replace the ancient bulbs in the ceiling lights (200 percent brighter at a third of the cost of the bulbs we'd been using, and a 15-year life span to boot!). And, they would be installed in time for the upcoming Sunday worship.

A great effort from the trustee to make something happen and get the job done!

The following Sunday morning the sanctuary was bathed in a new glow; not a glaring light in any way, but a wonderfully appropriate brightness that accentuated the beautiful stained glass windows. The pulpit and the nave revealed a new level of detail. Importantly, the pastor could be seen more easily. It wasn't a spotlight type of effect on her but rather a subtle backlighting that added a glow to her presence, and thus her presentation and message.

On this particular Sunday the "light of the new day" was an energizing addition to the experience of being in our church. From my seat I heard someone say: "Hey isn't the sanctuary brighter today? It looks good!"

With the response from an adjacent parishioner: "Yes, you're right. I knew it felt different in here."

As moderator I felt a sense of satisfaction on many fronts: the quick call to action from the trustee in his communication with the board and the electrician concerning the issue; his follow through on executing the recommended plan; and his diligence in getting the project done right away, with little fuss.

The new lighting created a warmer experience and showcased our beautiful church. My satisfaction and enthusiasm carried over to my anticipation for the coffee hour where I was sure we'd hear more compliments. As I descended the stairs to the fellowship hall I was motivated to talk to as many people as I could about how great the new lighting looked—how it added to the ambience of the sanctuary, the spirit of the sermon, and the entire participation in the worship service.

Three steps into the fellowship hall—and twenty steps from the coffee I was so looking forward to—I encountered a couple who'd been coming to the church for about two years.

"Good morning!" I said enthusiastically. "Aren't the new lights nice?" I waited to hear them tell me how much they liked our improved lighting.

BANG!

Their response deflated my enthusiasm as quickly as a needle popping a birthday balloon.

"Actually, the new lights gave me a headache. I really don't like them."

"I'm so sorry to hear that." I felt deflated.

The rest of the conversation was perfunctory, because I wasn't going to say the lights would be changed. Their facial expressions convinced me that on this day, at this particular moment, I would not be able to completely satisfy them. I could only act sympathetic.

This was a reality check moment for me and a good learning experience. The exchange alerted me to the fact that I can't make everyone happy all the time. One member thinks the sanctuary is too dark, another says it's too bright. The situation underscored my innocence to the reality of how church life replicates real life. Why should it be any other way?

> If the right intent is there—go for it. Just don't expect that every positive move will be received and accepted as such.

I've since heard that the music is occasionally too loud; that it's difficult to hear some of the speakers and readers; that we should add certain elements to the worship service, and absolutely take away others that have been part of the service for years. I now realize there will always be give-and-take to the process of growing a church and making it better for all involved. The ability to persevere in the face of occasional disapproval from church members is an offshoot of a church family existing and learning together.

If the right intent is there—go for it. Just don't expect, as I did, that every positive move will be received and accepted as such. The footnote to the story is the couple shortly thereafter decided to leave the church. They "weren't feeling it." I just hope it wasn't the lighting!

Jane's Commentary

I am always amazed at how much some church people dislike change—even positive change, such as an improvement to the lighting in the sanctuary. Any modification, good or bad, can upset a person who hates change. It is especially difficult to have people in the church who hate change, because a growing church is a changing church. New people mean new ideas, and that means change. When you're excited to grow your church and someone does or says something that makes it feel as if all of your efforts are for nothing—that can be very discouraging. It makes you wonder about any and all future efforts to improve things.

When a church begins to grow and members dig in their heels and rally against all the changes, you simply have to ignore them. That isn't easy, but you have to cheerfully persist. The key to survival for the pastor of a growing church is to keep pushing forward and not be overly affected by negative comments such as "the lights are too bright." Don't let the opinions of a few—no matter how persistent or loud—make you stop improving and growing your church. And don't let it stop you from actively welcoming new people.

Sometimes all you can do is ignore the complaints and remind yourself, "This is all worth it to have a thriving church."

Making it Happen Guidelines Worksheet

List three aspects of your church that need to change. They can be physical, emotional or spiritual.

1. _____

2. _____

3. _____

Identify one person in the congregation who might be an ally in change. Ask them to lunch. Explain what you need.

_____

Chapter Fourteen
Overdoing the Extravagant Welcome

By Jane

The woman greeted us almost before we stepped through the church door. My husband and I were "between" churches, as I had accepted a new call, but hadn't started working at the new church. In the meantime, we thought we'd try a church near our new house in our new neighborhood. When we stepped into the lobby we were immediately "swooped" upon by an elderly woman wearing a badge that read "Deacon." Her overwhelming approach to us made it seem as if she hadn't seen a visitor in years. And looking around, I had to wonder if maybe that was the case.

This was early on in my ministry before I'd done much work teaching church groups to appropriately greet and welcome visitors. I later began to call this experience of the overzealous church greeter the "welcome gush," which like any onslaught, is urgent and desperate and leaves those hit by it startled. Few visitors want to "stand out" so quickly. Usually if someone is attending a church for the first time, they're hesitant. Maybe they just want to test out the idea of church at all. Or they want to see if the church is "better" than it was 20 years ago when they were last in a church. Or maybe they're seeking a spiritual or emotional answer to a pressing issue. Perhaps they wandered in while they waited for The Gap to open its doors (I had a friend who started attending church because the department store where she wanted to shop didn't open until 10:00 AM. The church down the block started at 9:00 AM. She went inside). Whatever the reason, a visitor wants a warm welcome—and then to be left alone.

A church member of mine told this story at our prospective members meeting. He said he tried another church nearby, but was accosted in the narthex by two greeters, a gift bag, a pledge card, and a name tag. He never made it into the pews, but left his gift bag on a table and escaped to the parking lot. The welcome committee members at that church were diligent in their goals of "welcoming each person," but they may have overdone it.

The most important thing to do in your initial greeting is to warmly say "good morning," hand the visitor an order of worship (if that's what your church uses), and then direct them toward the pews. Once you do that, your job is done—at least for a while.

The amazing thing is how few churches can pull this off. A simple greeting becomes either an onslaught of over-the-top welcome, or it isn't there at all and leaves visitors thinking they've entered a private club and no one taught them the secret handshake.

Michael was one of our most loyal and enthusiastic members. I noticed that every Sunday he slipped in just before the choir's anthem. He missed the announcements, the call to worship, and the passing of the peace. The strange thing was that I knew he was at the church because, as one of our trustees, he came early to turn on the lights and heat. Michael was reliable and wonderful—the kind of church member every pastor wants. So one day, I was interested when he explained why he came late to the worship service. "Pastor," he said. "I like to wait until the passing of the peace is ended." It turns out that three other church members also waited in the back until the mayhem of the passing of the peace was over.

Lots of churches do a passing of the peace and if your church loves it, that ritual will be hard to change. But think about it— the passing of the peace ritual can be difficult for new people. Imagine wanting to just slip in and "see" what church is like and then being forced to exuberantly mingle with a crowd of people you aren't even sure you want to be with. I convinced my congregation to take their "meet and greet" downstairs following the service at coffee hour. Now, Michael can be found sitting in the pew early during the prelude.

As our churches get smaller, our desire to build them up gets bigger. That isn't a bad impulse, but it can work against us. First-time visitors sometimes find themselves asked to do everything from joining the choir to sponsoring next week's coffee hour in the fellowship hall (even though they may have just learned what a fellowship hall is). And as tempting as it may be, don't hand them a pledge card. We tend to overwhelm and drain the life out of visitors. We need to let them be visitors. They did not come to worship to find a new set of friends, a volunteer assignment, and one more place to commit their money.

> As our churches get smaller, our desire to build them up gets bigger. That isn't a bad impulse, but it can work against us.

I began this chapter with a description of the visit my husband and I made to a new church. I'd been hired by the church across town where I would start in two weeks. The church people were incredibly welcoming at the church we were visiting (too welcoming as I already said), until they realized who I was. At some point in the pastor's sermon, he looked out and said "let us welcome Pastor Willan, she will be starting at the UCC Church as their new pastor." Not only was I not ready to be introduced to the congregation—I had slipped in hoping to actually worship as a full participant since I would soon be immersed in leading a congregation. But the feeling in the room of disappointment mixed with immediate disinterest, was palpable. My husband and I were no longer potential members, no longer important. So much for the extravagant welcome.

When we welcome people into our sanctuary, we need to forget how badly we want to build up our membership. It isn't about us. We need to engage in true hospitality. In other words, "We're glad you are here because you've joined us in the worship and praise of God." If visitors decide to stay and become a member of the Board, lead the youth group, bake pies for the fund-raiser, and go to Annual Meeting as a delegate—that's great. But if they just want to slip in, listen to the prayers and sermon, engage in the beauty of the music, and then slip out again refreshed to their very souls—that's good too.

Peter's Commentary

When it comes to interacting with visitors at our church, I've become hyper-sensitive to the delicate balance between showing genuine appreciation and interest in their attendance, versus overwhelming them with an extravagant welcome. Writing a book on church growth will do that to you.

> No matter why they came, a warm, genuine welcome goes a long way in helping people feel recognized and included.

Fortunately, more and more visitors have been appearing on Sunday morning. And now each Sunday I fully expect to see a new face, or three, or four in the crowd. It's quite exciting. I always wonder what exactly brought them. What have they heard about the church? What have they heard about the pastor? What do they seek? Or, perhaps their attendance has nothing to do with any of those things. No matter why they came, a warm, genuine welcome goes a long way in helping people feel recognized and included.

At a recent coffee hour I walked up to a couple I'd seen perhaps once before. While we hadn't had an in-depth conversation during our initial interaction, I felt comfortable about approaching them again to say hello and perhaps ask another question or two, perhaps something along the line of "It's nice to see you both again, what brings you here today?" Much to my surprise and delight, they told me "We've decided we're going to join the church!" It was a thrilling moment and I commented how exciting it would be to have them as members. They had seen how the pastor leads and how the congregation is energized about where we are, and where we're going. They were able to make that all-important decision relatively early.

We didn't scare them away with an over-the-top welcome. Instead we showcased what the church is all about—and with a message of appreciation and inclusion, we invited them to make their own decision and join us at their own pace.

So take a measured, confident approach to this aspect of church growth instead of overdoing the extravagant welcome. We are excited that they, and many others, are deciding to make this church their spiritual home, and we believe our approach has a lot to do with it.

Making it Happen Worksheet

What's your process for welcoming visitors to your church?

_____

_____

_____

In what ways could it be overdone?

_____

_____

_____

What could you do to tone it down?

_____

_____

_____

Keep a list of visitors. How often does a visitor return?

_____

_____

_____

_____

_____

_____

Chapter Fifteen
Prospecting Procrastination

By Jane

Peter stepped into my office one afternoon at the church and asked in his usual enthusiastic voice, "So … how are the calls going?" Peter's inquiry was in response to a goal I'd set a month earlier to make "cold calls" to church members who had lapsed in their membership. In other words, members who stopped coming to church.

In some cases we knew why they stopped, but with other members, not so much. Church members drift away for a variety of reasons. Most literature says that when a church member leaves, the pastor shouldn't expend a lot of energy to get them back. It's almost always a waste of time and effort. But that was a theory I just couldn't accept. I believed that if I tried, I might at least regain a few. I asked the congregation to email the names of people they knew who had left the church during the past five years. Although I expected a list of names, I had no idea how big that list would be. At least fifty individuals and couples were identified by church members in emails, notes left on my desk, and names told to me while standing in line at the grocery store. My secretary took the jumble of names and compiled them into an alphabetized list, complete with phone numbers and even a brief description of why that particular person or couple might have left the church.

Nothing stood in the way of my tackling the list and making the fifty calls. I set a goal of so many calls per week and even the day of the week I would devote to the task. So you would think this would be a fairly straightforward task. It wasn't.

When Peter asked me how the calls were going, I hated to tell him. "Well," I said. "I've been so busy with stewardship and..." I had no real answer. For one thing, so much depends on membership growth, especially in a small- to medium-sized church like mine. If I wanted to work on stewardship (or anything else for that matter), I should have been enthusiastically

> For a pastor, at least a pastor like me, cold calls were the furthest thing from my mind. But the people on my list to call had deliberately left the church, meaning a personal invitation from the pastor was necessary.

making calls. But I had conveniently found other things to do, and the neatly organized list got buried on my desk.

Peter looked at me quizzically. I could tell he wondered why I hadn't even started. Peter is a salesman, so making cold calls is second nature to him. For a pastor, at least a pastor like me, cold calls were the furthest thing from my mind. My idea of attracting new members has always been less direct. A warm greeting at the door of the church, a good sermon, a heartfelt invitation to coffee hour, and let the cards fall where they may. But that whole approach (if you can even call it an approach—it is better termed a default) was obviously not working. First, it depended entirely on the idea that people were already in the church door, looking for a pew, and standing to sing songs they probably already knew. This is a passive attitude I dislike, and yet I had clearly adopted it.

The people on my list to call had deliberately left the church, meaning a personal invitation from the pastor was necessary. I needed to pick up the phone and make those calls. And so I did. Partly out of pressure from Peter's polite though confused reaction, and partly because I felt like a church growth loser. And a very small part of me wanted to see if I could do it. Could I actually call a person I'd never met, who had something against the church and who probably wanted to hear from me as much as I wanted to hear from a telemarketer at dinner time?

I started with the name at the top of my list: a woman who left because she felt the church had pressured her into joining and running committee after committee. The secretary put in quotes that this woman announced to another church member, she had "had it." I sat staring at her name and number for quite a while. I decided to do some quick research on making cold calls. Note, however, that the calls I was attempting were not actually cold—since the people at one point did have a connection to the church. They were more like "lukewarm calls."

I googled *cold calls* and was surprised at the plethora of websites, blogs, and entire books that addressed cold calling. I read several pages before I clicked off the computer and just picked up the phone. Although all the experts said you needed to have a script—in fact several scripts, depending on what you encountered in the call—I couldn't do that. I could not come up with a canned response. I decided to wing it—something I seldom do.

With trepidation and the promise to myself that I only had to do one call and I could quit, I listened as the woman's phone rang, secretly hoping for an answering machine. She answered. I started by introducing myself and, to my pleasant surprise, winging it had been the best decision. My pastoral voice kicked in and I found myself genuinely interested in the woman's story. I said a few welcoming and introductory things and then let her talk. She seemed willing to discuss why she left the church (just letting people talk wasn't in my original plan—I was going to wow people with my "sale" of the church and myself and they would be dying to come back). Instead, I listened. We ended the call with the offer that she would come back and "check things out since surely they have changed." I felt jubilant. I did it!

I quickly went down my list, meeting different levels of success. Some people immediately told me they weren't interested. Others were a little lukewarm, but still easy to talk with and perhaps might show interest in the future. But

> My advice when prospecting is to never get discouraged and never give up. Sometimes it just takes time.

about 25 percent of my calls brought promises of returning to church that next Sunday. It was a Thursday. On Sunday, I confidently stood at the front door of the church, with a stack of bulletins in my hand and a welcoming smile. I was ready to greet my new 25 percent.

None of them came.

Church began and ended with the usual handful of faithful people. Hymns were sung, the sermon preached, the collection taken, and the spirit acknowledged. Without my promised people.

I didn't do any cold calls that week. Which was too bad, because on the next Sunday two of my "called people" came to church. Not the entire group, but two new members was a promising start.

I have continued the calls and expanded my list from lapsed members to truly cold calls to people and families who moved into the area. I get a list from a local realtor's office and start calling. We also send a follow up letter.

Interestingly, no one comes to church immediately upon invitation. It takes a few weeks or longer. I'm not sure why, but it does. I have learned to change my expectations. Just because I'm excited doesn't mean they are. My advice when prospecting is to never get discouraged and never give up. Sometimes it just takes time. And that's okay. As long as you are calling and trying, you will grow your church.

Growing a church cannot be a hit and miss project. It needs to be as big a priority as getting your sermon done. Think about how much time you spend on your sermon each week. What if you devoted that much time to church growth—to deliberate growth activities such as cold calls, letter writing, coffee with those people who have visited once or twice, organizing a welcoming committee, and evaluating the physical structure of the church for welcoming potential? How much time do you spend on your sermon? Five hours? Ten hours? Pledge to devote the same amount of time to growth activities. Think of prospecting as equal to the sermon in importance.

Don't procrastinate. Get started today.

Peter's Commentary

Here's how to get started: For the next two weeks, challenge yourself to commit one hour each week to phone calls, using Jane's messaging approach. You can reasonably project that for every two hours of dedicated prospecting you'll find two or three prospective members. Aren't those people worth two hours of your time?

I suggest using a worksheet like this to track your progress:

Day/Time: _____

Called and left messages with:

1. _____

2. _____

3. _____

4. _____

5. _____

6. _____

7. _____

8. _____

9. _____

10. _____

Called and spoke with:

1. _____

    Next Steps:_____

2. _____

    Next Steps:_____

3. _____

    Next Steps:_____

4. _____

    Next Steps:_____

I predict the success you experience during this two week period will propel you to make these phone calls a regular part of your work growing your church.

While we're on the topic of prospecting, remember that wherever you are, anyone you meet could be a prospecting opportunity. Always carry business cards containing the church information and your contact information. Whether you use a smart phone, a tablet, or a trusty notepad, have a means to record your interactions and note phone numbers and email addresses of the people you meet. You'll be glad you did. There's a good chance that someone you meet in this fashion is a person you'll reach out to at a later date.

Finally, I loved seeing the different expressions on Reverend Jane's face before she made her first prospecting calls and then after the fact.

Chapter Sixteen

*Using Missions to Grow Your Church:
Jesus Won't Mind.
You're Still Helping People*

By Jane

"It isn't that I don't want these people in church, it's just that when I look around, they don't look like us. You know, the old faces." That comment was in response to a new outreach program at my church. A local facility for developmentally disabled adults was bringing a van of residents to church every Sunday. The once empty front pew was now filled, since they all liked to sit together and loved being in the front.

"I've heard things about him, Pastor. I'm not going to say what exactly, but I don't think you want him to have a key to our church." This comment was in response to giving a key to a new church member named Frank. Frank was nearly homeless and lived here and there around town. He joined the church and, recognizing a need, offered to open the building every Sunday morning. Frank was the most faithful church opener I've ever had. He not only turned on lights, adjusted the thermostat, and unlocked doors. He also made the coffee. But it was a constant fight to keep certain church members from taking away his key to the building.

"All I can say is—you're trading $50.00 members for $5.00 members." This was said to me at a board meeting when it was announced that people who ate at our soup kitchen were to be welcomed "upstairs" to the service on Sunday. A few of them had started joining the church and participating in the adult Sunday school class.

If you want to grow your church, one of the best actions you can take is serving the low income members of your community. Three things are likely to happen. First, you will know you are indeed following the Gospel. Second, you will start to welcome the very people you "help" to join in the life of your church. And third, people who are not impressed with organized religion will sit up and start paying attention to what your church is doing. I guarantee people will join you simply because they've finally found a church that "does something."

> If you want to grow your church, one of the best actions you can take is serving the low income members of your community. I encourage you to take the challenge and the risk of truly welcoming all people.

The question is, do you really want the disenfranchised in your pews? We're fine with the homeless and nearly homeless people sitting in the basement eating our free community meal. But do you want them in your pews? And the better question, do you want them serving as deacons, board members, and delegates to the annual meeting? If you want to look around and see lawyers, doctors, teachers, and other professionals in your sanctuary and on your boards and committees, then I say, "Go for it."

But I encourage you to take the challenge and the risk of truly welcoming all people. We all say we welcome everyone, but if we do, why aren't our pews filled with the very people who most need the support of the church community?

Here are some ways you can be a church that uses mission to grow:

1. Open the doors of the church to the community for a free meal one day a week. Sounds like a lot of work, right? It is and it isn't. Find a church member who will really "own" the project and it will be easier than you think.

2. Call the local homeless shelter and ask if you can come on Sunday morning and give residents a ride to church. The same for half-way houses, treatment centers, and nursing homes. Church isn't just for those who can drive.

3. Start a food pantry in your church. Stock it with donated food and a few volunteers. Encourage people to come as often as they want. We have one and our motto is "All the food you want, all the time." Put no restrictions on who gets food or how often. Extravagant generosity goes a lot further than trying to decide who really deserves those cans of creamed corn.

There are many reasons to open the doors of your church to serve the community, but you can also think of mission as also a way to grow the church.

Peter's Commentary

The snow started falling early in the morning on this particular Thursday—another storm in the seemingly endless stream of dangerous storms and road conditions battering New England. By 2 p.m. the snow was falling at the rate of an inch an hour.

"I don't think you'll be going tonight," I said to Mary, as she put the lasagna she had prepared for the residents of Dismas House in Worcester, Massachusetts into the oven. Dismas House is a transitional facility that prepares people who've been incarcerated for re-entry into society. Mary's lasagna is incredible, and part of the reason I encouraged her to stay home was likely due to the fact I would get some of it.

"No, we're definitely going. Don will be driving and he has the four-wheel drive SUV, so we'll be fine." she replied. By 5 p.m. several more inches of snow covered the ground. On top of the 14 inches we received a few days earlier, this made travel especially tricky.

"Well, at least can I drive you up to the church?" I said.

"Yes, that would be helpful. Keep these trays flat in the back and support them on either side."

"Yes, dear."

The heat and aroma of lasagna punctuated the frigid temperatures in the car. The drive up to the church was quiet— there were no other cars on the road—and the fresh layers of snow suppressed the noise of the tires finding their grip. As we climbed the steep hill on Church Street I was now more worried about the trays of lasagna staying intact than the driving conditions. The inside of the car smelled like the finest Italian restaurant, and my stomach ached for the lasagna. We pulled into the church parking lot. Don was already there with his capable vehicle. Debbie, chair of the missions committee, was also there unloading the other elements of the meal into the SUV. The feast was prepared and ready to go! Off they went back down Church Street heading to Dismas House.

Due to Don's skillful driving they arrived safely, and on time, at their destination. The residents were waiting for them at the door and very happy to see them. "You shouldn't have come out in weather like this," one of them said to Mary. Yet, she told me later that she could tell he and the others were overjoyed to see them. For the next two hours, six members of our church enjoyed dinner with the residents.

By 8 p.m. the meal was finished, the residents had cleaned everything up, the casserole pans and dishes were back in Don's car, and the group headed back to the church. A few weeks later, two members of the group from Dismas came and spoke at a Sunday service. Their life stories were compelling tales of misfortune and bad decisions leading to further bad luck and misfortune, all helped through the efforts of Dismas House. They spoke of how their lives had been turned around by their faith and by people from the churches. The stories were moving and emotional—and to some in our congregation—educational as well.

We were also excited to see tangible results from this one mission outreach, one of many handled by the church, and the reality of how the church can truly help people in both our congregation and our wider community. Their stories and the open appreciation of our members who serve at Dismas House served as an inspiration for others to get involved and contribute. In many ways, the work at Dismas House formed a solid foundation from which to grow the church.

Efforts like these are rewarded in both anticipated and unexpected ways, especially in church growth.

Don't let anything get in the way of mission work. Just be ready to call on someone like Don in your congregation to skillfully pilot the SUV through the snow drifts.

Making it Happen Worksheet

List three ways you could open the doors of the church:

1. _____

2. _____

3. _____

Identify one ally in the church who might "own" one of the three outreach projects.

_____

Chapter Seventeen
Riding the Wave of Disapproval

By Jane

"Really, Pastor. I think you need to let the dust settle." These were the words of my church moderator. The church treasurer standing nearby vigorously nodded agreement, frowning at the same time. I knew that tone of voice; I had heard it before. This was complete disapproval. The two church leaders didn't like the many changes the church board and I were making.

We stood in the newly repainted and decorated narthex of the church. Gone were the old, tired couch and chairs that had been donated a decade ago. The pastel print of the lighthouse that hung on the walls so long you could see its faded imprint on the dreary paint, was replaced by warm colors and splashy art; the new carpet squares still had that new-carpet-smell; and a large, previously empty space had been arranged with carefully placed café tables and barstools. The new narthex had the look of a trendy coffee shop. Inviting, contemporary, and alive.

Those cosmetic changes were difficult enough for the moderator and treasurer, but the changes they were referred to now were more upsetting than cosmetic. The church had started the process of Open and Affirming—a celebration in the United Church of Christ that makes public and deliberate a congregation's welcoming of all LGBT people. Open and Affirming in the United Church of Christ is not just "love the sinner, hate the sin," but a full embrace of acceptance extending far beyond tolerance. That was a huge problem for these two church members.

Time to let the dust settle. My response? "What would it look like with settled dust?" Not a terribly sensitive answer, but I was tired of the struggle to stop the movement of growth and change that was beginning to define and invigorate this particular church. Settled dust did not much appeal to me and it certainly didn't sound like the hallmark of a growing church.

Many parishioners feel anxious with the changes brought about by a church in the process of growth. They may feel nervous about change itself, or they may feel their own power and control being peeled away. Either response to change seems to always result in a universal need to tell the pastor to, "slow things down." I've been told "you need to take a step back" and another time, to "calm down." At a board meeting one parishioner said, "No new programs!" That was at my first church and I remember pondering why anyone would oppose new programs.

All of this is what I call the wave of disapproval. If you plan on growing your church, you need to learn to ride it out. Not cave into it, not backtrack, but cheerfully grit your teeth and keep moving forward.

The first step in living through disapproval is to learn to make changes without asking permission. Good leaders do not ask permission. They also don't try to make everyone happy or blame themselves when everyone isn't happy. I don't mean you should be a tyrant, but don't be a pushover either. If you see an appropriate change your church needs—anything from redecoration to an investment review—you need to push ahead and not let your fear of approval hold you back or keep you from making the right decision.

I'm not saying you should ignore the polity of your church. Our churches have protocol for every major decision and those protocols should be followed. The decisions most likely done by proper protocol are things like budgets, nominations to committees, and use of the church building. All decisions of that sort should come before the governing board and should be done by committee.

If you're in a congregational church as I am, you also know that some decisions come before the entire congregation: for example, hiring a pastor is certainly subject to a congregational vote, as well as the fulfillment of capital projects. All of these things are properly outside the sole decision of the pastor. However, when you find the governing board voting on whether or not the youth group can have a bulletin board in the fellowship hall, you know you're You will never grow your church if you require permission and approval at every turn. in trouble. Not every decision needs group approval. The pastor needs to plunge ahead on her own sometimes. Unfortunately, many pastors seem paralyzed by their own systems of governance and are afraid to do anything without a vote or formal permission of everyone.

Why is this? I think most people who go into ministry are inherently and genuinely nice. They care about the feelings of others. They worry when people in their churches feel marginalized or ignored. All of this is good and probably makes for excellent pastoral care. But a true agent of change does not need or want permission to do everything. Nor is a true agent of change swayed by popular opinion. You will never grow your church if you require permission and approval at every turn.

If you know you're the kind of pastor who's uncomfortable with disapproval, then you will have to practice taking action without permission. Keep reminding yourself that if you wait for everyone to "have a say" or "get on board" or be given a "voice" you will never grow your church in the way it could grow. Give up your need to be liked. It will make you a better pastor in the long run.

When I first came to the Congregational Church of Grafton, we were mailing out 230 print newsletters each month. The postage, paper, ink, and labor stretched the limits of our tight budget. I looked through the addresses of the people getting the monthly church newsletter and determined we could email at least 200 of the newsletters and send out as few as thirty hardcopies. **This could save several hundreds of dollars per year.** However, raising the subject with the governing board resulted in a firestorm of opinion. A few board members were very much in favor of emailing the newsletter and several were adamantly against it. We never reached a consensus on what to do.

A month went by and it was time to send out the newsletter again. When the church secretary asked me what she should do, I told her to send out 200 electronic copies and send the rest to those she thought did not have email—to about thirty older church members. **I nervously waited for the response of the congregation and to my surprise—there was none.** People quickly adjusted to getting their newsletters by email, and a few who received it by snail mail asked to be put on the email list. My decision to "just do it" paid off. Certainly not all changes done by the pastor will be so easy, but you might be surprised by how quickly parishioners will adjust when given no choice.

So why do pastors want so badly for everyone to weigh in before they make a change? Because that makes our jobs easier. We convince ourselves that we're being democratic or fair, but we're really being a bit cowardly. Perhaps cowardly is overstating it. Perhaps a better way of saying it is that we're taking the path of least resistance—a path that never leads to growth.

In one of my churches we drastically changed the way in which memorial money was distributed. After serving the church for only a few months, it became obvious to me and the church treasurer that the committee handling money from memorials was reluctant to ever spend it. They only allowed memorial money to be spent after a complicated process of permissions and correspondence from the family who gave the money—even if the amount was only a few hundred dollars. And this process, without meaning to, encouraged families to place restrictions on even small amounts of money. As a result, the memorial committee at this church held the money "hostage" (my word, certainly not theirs) and it sat for years in a checking account.

The treasurer was in agreement with me on the problems with this process and we worked for months with the memorial committee to change the policy and make the spending of memorial money more effective by freeing it from all restrictions. We met with members of the committee, discussed, explained, and listened. In the end, we put forth a proposal to the governing board. Their vote put into practice a new and much more effective way of using memorial funds.

Did all the listening and gathering of opinion and feelings help make this change easier? No. In the end, I wonder if we introduced more controversy than if we had just pushed the proposal through to start with. If you and the leaders of your church agree on a policy change, I suggest that you *not* gather every opinion and consider every nuance. Just do it.

Also, any change in policy or new program or paint color can be changed back if it doesn't work out. Nothing is written in stone. If you have an idea of how to improve the life and health of your congregation—I suggest trying it even if every detail is not ironed out. You can always tweak it later.

Or you can decide it didn't work and do something else.

Remember, if you are not held hostage by the fear of disapproval then you are truly liberated to serve your church as it should be served.

Finally, if you're going to step up and really make changes in your church for its growth and health, then you also have to

be accountable and responsible

> If you are not held hostage by the fear of disapproval then you are truly liberated to serve your church as it should be served.

for your actions. If something was your idea, own it. But don't back down because people are pressuring you. Back down only when you think you were wrong. Never be afraid to be wrong. Never be afraid to be right.

If you want to grow your church you will have to institute change not everyone likes. Your church is not growing for a reason. Find out what it is and force a change. And then hang in there until it's done.

Peter's Commentary

Jane said in Chapter One, "I consider myself in sales. I'm in sales and service."

Because I've worked in sales for many years, Jane's narrative brings to mind the elements of professional, integrity-based selling. The ability to lead the congregation in new directions occasionally requires a pastor's ability to convince those who disagree. Just like sales!

Confidence is required to convince naysayers that you want to go in a different direction, and then move in that direction regardless of whether or not everyone gives you a green light.

This doesn't in any way mean you're bulldozing your way to decision-making by disregarding people's opinions. Rather, it means you're judiciously analyzing the impact and results of your decisions and carefully conveying the message to those involved.

Jane's decision at our church to begin emailing the newsletter despite the protestations of a vocal minority is a case in point. As Jane said:

"Never be afraid to be wrong."

"Never be afraid to be right."

As I see it, make sure you fully understand the value and benefits of the position you want to take—and then go for it!

Making it Happen Guidelines Worksheet

Identify a change you'd like to implement that may bring disapproval from the congregation.

_____

_____

Who will be your worst opponents?

_____

To whom can you turn for support?

_____

What is the worst thing that can happen?

_____

_____

_____

Chapter Eighteen

*Letting Go of the Praise Band and
Learning to Love the Hymnbook Again*

By Jane

"You'll never grow your church without a praise band. You will certainly never attract young people." My colleague was adamant and sounded like a true authority on the subject. I was unconvinced. After repeated and unsuccessful attempts to introduce "praise songs" and an even less successful attempt to pull together enough musicians for an actual praise band, my congregation had embraced the hymnbook all over again. And even in the light of my colleague's dire predictions, our church grew.

This near-obsession with having a praise band (and if you have one—more power to you) or at least a hodge-podge group of people with guitars and a random drum set or two, reminds me of the "get rid of the pews" obsession of the 1970s. I enjoy a praise band some of the time—especially a good one. But is it a prerequisite to growing a church? No. Are you doomed if you don't have one? Not at all. And is it the band that attracts young people? Not necessarily. We need to give our millennial generation a little more credit than thinking they come to church to hear a group of middle-aged people play guitar and sing a repetitive verse into a microphone.

But the two biggest obstacles for most small to medium size churches in starting and maintaining a praise band are lack of funds and talent. These churches can't afford the bands and their congregations aren't large enough to provide talented volunteer musicians.

The problem with wanting to revitalize your church is that it's easy to jump on every band wagon (sorry for the near-pun) just because someone out there tells you it will grow your church. An urgency exists in small and or declining churches that the quick fix of a praise band seems to answer. It may be, but it probably isn't. Unless you have the resources—financial reserve, actual musicians, and a good sound system—you are not going to have success with your newly formed praise band. You will need to win over reluctant members as well as impress those who know what the music is supposed to sound like. A good praise band is hard to create and sustain. You'll need a talented leader, regular weekly practices, and dedicated musicians.

Remember, a mediocre praise band is not better than none at all. It's worse.

So what can you do?

First, stop thinking about the traditions of the past as an automatic hindrance to growth and make the music you already experience better and a little more diverse. What is good about the music you already have? Can your church commit to a better organist, a more dedicated choir, a director of music who's willing to try new songs that are still within your congregation's comfort zone? Good music is essential. It may not necessarily grow your church. But bad music is sure to kill it.

> Good music is essential. It may not necessarily grow your church. But bad music is sure to kill it.

My stepdaughter is a millennial. She is smart, independent, lives in a large city—and she's looking for a church. When I asked what she was looking for, I expected to hear something different from what I heard. She grew up in a traditional Lutheran church. I expected her to want contemporary music—a praise band at the very least—a youthful congregation, and a young pastor. I asked about her requirements for a new church. She said, "I want a church that does something in the world. And a worship service that is meaningful, not stupid."

> Church music should not be "something for everyone." This attitude tends to dilute and weaken.

I pressed her further. "So what kind of music would you want?" I asked.

"Well, I guess I like songs that I know. Something I can at least sing to," she said.

"Do you mean hymns? Out of a hymnbook?"

"Well, yes. Church music."

"What about a praise band?"

"No. Those are always so lame. If I'm going to church, I want it to at least seem like church."

With that our conversation ended. Those of us who buy into the "all young adults want is praise music" or "the only way to attract youth is to get rid of the organ and the hymns" may not be as smart as we think.

So if a praise band isn't going to save us, as far as music is concerned, what is? Good music. Good music that is a nice mix of old and new, taize and hymnody, jazz and Gregorian. Not a crazy hodge-podge, but a sensible and reasonable blend.

Church music should not be "something for everyone"—a huge mistake because there will be no end to it. An attitude of "something for everyone" tends to dilute and weaken. Clearly the purpose of music in the worship service is to enhance the experience of worship: to bring people into the presence of

God. If that's what the music in your church is doing, then it's working.

Think of ways to improve your ability to accomplish that specific purpose. You actually do not have to make it appealing to all ages and all people. Your first responsibility is to make it worshipful.

Let go of the praise band and learn to love the hymnbook again.

Peter's Commentary

From my perspective, besides a dynamite sermon, nothing draws me into the spirit of worship quite like the music. Whether it's the power of the choir singing in unison, the strength of a soloist, or the crescendo of the organ during the descant, it's wonderful to feel moved by music in the sanctuary.

A few years ago, while attending Easter Sunday at a church in Connecticut, our extended family was staying at my in-laws' house. The large group required three vehicles—my car and two minivans—to ferry everyone to church for the service. We sequenced the departures according to how quickly everyone could get ready. The first minivan would leave at 10:30, the second at 10:40, and my car would be the last to leave at 10:45.

As I dutifully sat in my car in the driveway at 10:45, waiting for the final two members of the family to emerge from the house, I was able to reflect on the anticipation and excitement of hearing my favorite hymn "Christ the Lord Has Risen Today" resounding through the beautiful sanctuary. This hymn always made me an emotional wreck and I expected to have tears running down my face. I could hardly wait!

But, the two remaining family members hadn't yet appeared.

By 10:53 I knew we might be late for the eleven o'clock service.

At 10:55, I jumped out of the car and raced into the house. "Hey, let's go!" I shouted. "We've got to go right now!"

After a quick search, I realized the house was empty. The digital clock on the television in the living area of the third floor now read 11:00 a.m.

And then it hit me. I was going to miss "Christ the Lord Has Risen Today." I ran back downstairs, jumped in the car, and raced to the church.

As this was the second service on Easter Sunday, parking was at a premium and the likelihood of getting a space anywhere near church was impossible. I was relegated to parking in an office park about one third of mile from the church. I raced along the concrete sidewalk, my Sunday shoes making it harder to run.

At 11:12 I reached the balcony where the family—all of them—were seated. The look on Mary's face said it all.

I had missed my favorite Easter hymn.

The two family members I'd been waiting for had slipped into the second minivan without telling me. They didn't understand I was waiting for them. They were sorry, and I was disappointed.

The impact of that single hymn carries me (almost) through the year. That's the emotional force of music, loving the hymnbook, and—as Jane says "bringing people into the presence of God." Music can do this every week, above and beyond Easter Sunday.

Just make sure no one's left behind in the driveway on Sunday morning!

Making it Happen Guidelines Worksheet

Does music in your church enhance the experience of
worship? If not, why?

List ten ways you wish you could improve music's impact.

1. _____

2. _____

3. _____

4. _____

5. _____

6. _____

7. _____

8. _____

9. _____

10. _____

Do children contribute to the music experience?

_____

Do non-member, professional musicians contribute to the
experience?

_____

Does the congregation contribute/participate in the music
experience?

_____

Chapter Nineteen

Grow Our Church, Pastor,
but Don't Make Us Change

By Jane

Everyone wants their church to grow. No one wants it to change. As a pastor, you must constantly initiate, facilitate, and encourage change. Sometimes you will gently tweak it along; other times you'll drive it like a freight train. Leading your congregation to change is not going to be fun. Many people won't like the change and will resent your actions. But growth and change always go hand in hand, and if you are not an agent of change in your church, then you are contributing to its decline. Without significant change, few churches will grow. And once they do begin growing, the changes new members bring can be extraordinary.

With new people come new ideas, new power systems, new committee chairs, and new questions with new answers. All of this creates a terrible dilemma for an institution that seems to shake in its boots about change. In the end, churches would rather die than change. And many do.

New people pose a threat to the way things have always been. The very thing you want in your church—new members—creates trepidation for some long-term members. Often the majority of people love seeing fresh faces sitting in the pews. But it isn't the majority that can sour a congregation—it's the difficult minority. And as pastor, your job is to get a handle on the negativity. When new people are seen as challenges or made to feel their ideas are suspect, then you must step in.

In my last church, a new couple joined the church. They were long-term residents of the town and well-liked. They looked like everyone else in the room and I certainly didn't anticipate any issues or problems from others in the congregation. But the new couple wanted to start a coffee hour immediately following church on Sundays. They were surprised that we didn't already have a coffee hour. I loved the idea and told them to go for it. What could be controversial or difficult about gathering for coffee on Sunday mornings?

However, some long-term members were upset. Church members came to me and said things like "this will never work" and "no one will come, Pastor" and the inevitable, "we tried this once and it didn't work." As the first coffee hour drew near, other issues were raised, such as, "Who will pay for the paper napkins and plates. What about all the extra coffee? Is the kitchen committee expected to absorb the cost?" One church member suggested I "needed to get this under control." I believe she meant get the new couple under control. I responded to the uproar by basically ignoring everyone. Coffee hour that first Sunday was packed and the fellowship hall was full every Sunday thereafter. The kitchen committee did absorb the cost of the coffee hour when they saw how much people enjoyed it and this hour turned into a wonderful fellowship opportunity for the entire church.

But what if I hadn't stuck up for the new couple? What if I allowed myself to cave under pressure?

(Let's face it—kitchen ladies can be persuasive.)

What if the new couple hadn't felt my support and the eventual support and gratitude of the congregation? They probably would not have joined the church, or if they had joined, they might have been hesitant to become engaged in the life of the congregation. New people have new ideas. Honor those ideas.

New people in your church mean the old people lose power. The issue is that simple. Some members are delighted to turn over the reins of power and go on to new things in the church or to sit back and take a break. Not everyone. Some people will do everything they can to undermine any innovation or idea or involvement of a new member. It's a little hard to believe the first time you witness it as a pastor, but unfortunately it can become commonplace.

As the pastor, you need to constantly be ready to affirm and support the ideas of a new member. This will not make you popular, especially if the person you're arguing with is an older person. The

> As the pastor, you need to constantly be ready to affirm and support the ideas of a new member.

WWII generation is not easy to convince. But if you want the invigorating life that only new members can bring, you'd better be prepared to go to bat for them. You need to have policies in place that allow relatively new people to serve on committees, be members of the governing board, and start new programs.

If your congregation is like mine—predominantly white and middle class, "new" may also mean people of color, people of a different socio-economic status, and people who are openly gay. Some congregations do not want to change with the environment. If the neighborhood was white and privileged in 1980, the church people who joined usually want it to stay white and privileged. I am at a progressive church in an area of economic privilege. So you can imagine my surprise when I got the text from a parishioner saying she was nervous about bringing her friend and friend's son to church. The friend is African American. I assured her it would be great to bring them—all people are welcome all the time. But I was a little stunned. Was this really an issue? The church member herself is not racist. And I would say the church as a whole is not racist. And yet, the question was asked, "Will it be okay to bring this family of color to our church?"

I think that question demonstrates how deeply and inherently our churches want to stay the same. If you are white, staying white is somehow preferable. Consequently, as a pastor you must call out racism for what it is and not go along happily as if it doesn't exist.

One reason congregations resist the change new members bring is that it takes them farther away from the past. Sometimes anything that removes us from the hey-day of the post WWII days is considered, well ... just wrong. And that's one more reason to recruit and encourage new members who are not chained to the past. They liberate us from the dependency on how things used to be when the pews were full. I'm not saying a connection to the past is all bad. Institutional history is important, but when the past becomes more real than the present, you have a problem. And it is probably a sign of slow death. As pastor, what do you do when your church is so cemented to the past that it cannot move forward even slightly?

Solution: Do everything you can to incorporate new members and encourage—even guarantee—their involvement.

Some people can't change and will leave. Let them go. Hanging on to members who consistently resist change, who do not feel they can welcome all people, who do not see themselves as part of the church as it is today, is a dangerous practice. Sometimes the church cannot grow until some people leave. You should

> Institutional history is important, but when the past becomes more real than the present, you have a problem. And it is probably a sign of slow death.

allow them to. Those people will never be happy under the leadership of a person who institutes and perpetuates change—especially the change brought about by new members. There are congregations that would rather retain one elderly, long-term member than welcome five new, young families. When you see your church members engaging in that kind of behavior, you need to intervene and put a stop to it. If you're hanging onto long-term members at the sacrifice of new members, you are no longer the church. You are a social club and you need to admit it.

The sad news: your church may do its best to drive out new people. This is both heart-breaking and infuriating to the pastor.

The young couple standing in the doorway of my office were clearly upset. "Come out here," the wife said to me. I left my desk and followed them outside. Scattered along the sidewalk in front of the church's large brick planter were flowers and plants. Each plant had been pulled up by its stems, clods of dirt clinging to the roots, petals and leaves quickly wilting in the hot sun.

The couple had recently joined the church and in their enthusiasm asked if they could work on the church gardens and lawn. I was ecstatic. Of course! After filling the planter with flowers they had gone home to get more gardening tools. In the meantime, an older couple (members of the church for forty years) drove by and saw the new flowers. They had been planting flowers in that planter for years (I didn't know this—it was my first spring at the church and as of yet, no one had done a thing to the planter). The older couple promptly stopped, got out, tore out the plants and flowers one by one, and tossed them on the sidewalk. Then they drove back home. After making a few phone calls, I found out what had happened. I was incredulous and went immediately to visit the older couple. When asked why they tore out the flowers, the older woman replied, "In my day, new people didn't just do things without permission."

Unfortunately, the older couple stayed in the church, but

eventually the young couple stopped coming. I visited and talked with them, but they had lost their enthusiasm. Incorporating new people isn't always this difficult, but when it is difficult, don't give up.

Peter's Commentary

"They've decided to leave the church" said the committee chairwoman

"Do we know why?" I asked. I was genuinely puzzled.

"They said they don't like the direction we're headed in."

The news reminded me of the time I put my bare foot into a moccasin and the wasp that had set up camp inside promptly stung my big toe. This sad news stayed with me for several days. You can't win them all, but any loss of membership creates a momentary period of reflection and disappointment.

What happened?

What did the church do wrong?

Was it the changes?

Upon deeper review of the situation, it turned out this particular family didn't agree with the flow of our worship service for a number of reasons. They didn't like a few new elements in the service and they were unhappy when a few other things were removed. So they're gone now. Not forgotten by any means, but not with us every Sunday.

However, it's okay.

They made a decision, and while I'm disappointed with the outcome, I respect it and trust they will find what they're looking for.

Solace comes for me in the realization that new members are now part of the congregation—people who are involved and contributing to the energy and spirit of the church. Together with the more tenured members, these new people are making things happen and revitalizing our services, the community we serve, and the missions outreach we're so proud of.

So, don't resist change.

Be prepared for legions of new members who will be sitting in the pews and give well wishes to the few who decide that change isn't for them.

Making it Happen Worksheet

What are the implied do's and don'ts in your church?

_____

_____

_____

Which of these would you change?

_____

Identify one ally in making this change.

_____

Chapter Twenty
People Matter, but So Do Numbers

By Peter

With 5,000 churches shutting their doors every year and many others teetering on the brink, survival can be tough, even in communities where a core of committed, spiritual people pour everything into their churches.

A few years ago, during a time of declining attendance and concern about the future, one of the most dedicated members of the church approached me one Sunday after church. Jon and his wife have since moved to New Jersey, but occasionally return to Grafton to check in with their former church family.

"I have a business opportunity and proposal for you," he said. "May I come and see you in your office one day this week?"

"Of course," I replied.

I was excited that someone in my church family and community was interested in my skills. In fact, I was so excited about it that I neglected to ask Jon what the project was about.

"Hey, Jon wants to meet with me this week," I told Mary that afternoon. "He says he has a project I might be interested in working on."

"That's good. What's the project?" she asked.

"I don't know, but he seems enthused about talking to me. And he's coming to my office to discuss it."

The following Thursday afternoon, the receptionist announced Jon had arrived and was waiting in one of the conference rooms. As I stepped out to join him, I was struck by the oddity of knowing someone only through church and then meeting them in my business environment.

I entered the conference room. Jon was looking as he always did on any Sunday morning, in a suit and tie. On the conference room table in front of him sat a notebook and a copy of my book on sales called *The Golden 120 Seconds of Every Sales Call*.

The meeting began.

"I'm not sure if you knew I went out and got a copy of your book and enjoyed reading it," Jon said.

"That's wonderful. Thank you on both counts!" I replied.

"The project I wanted to talk to you about—and gauge your interest in doing—has to do with the church."

That was unexpected.

Jon continued, "You discuss a lot of things in your book that are exactly what we should be doing in the church to stem the tide of people leaving, and to bring new people into membership. I think we need to do a better job of selling the church. We need your help to make that happen."

His thoughts came as a total surprise, yet I was enthralled and interested in getting involved. Why not? To a great degree, church leadership and growth involves being able to sell the church.

Pleased by my reaction and interest, Jon explained that the next stage in his project plan was to meet with the pastor and make sure she would be comfortable with this project. After that meeting, perhaps the three of us could make a plan on how to get it started.

I was excited, especially because at that time I wasn't a frequent attendee of church. Mary sang in the choir every week, but I often found other things to do on Sunday morning because the services left me unfulfilled and unmoved. Occasionally we would have a moment of enlightenment and energy, but for the most part I was part of a group within our church that felt disenfranchised.

I eagerly awaited Jon's follow-up call and started planning the early stages of the project.

But the project never got off the ground.

Jon called the following Tuesday and said, "She isn't interested. She said there's no place for sales in what we do. If people want to come to the church then they will."

And with a thud, we were done.

Jon was apologetic about taking my time and said he appreciated my interest. Yet, I could tell he was more disappointed than anything else. He had to resign himself to the fact that his efforts to stem the tide of declining attendance had been rejected.

> We had wonderful, caring, committed people in the church, but we were on a downward spiral. The first objective was to slow the rate of decline and reach stability.

We had wonderful, caring, committed people in the church, but we were on a downward spiral. Something would have to give if this 270-year-old institution was to survive. The people already in the church at that time absolutely "counted" and were a critical foundation, but the numbers were not enough to sustain this church. Finally, this realization triggered a series of events and actions—some wonderful and inspiring, a few challenging and difficult—to re-set the course of the church.

The first objective was to slow the rate of decline and reach stability. From there, we needed to establish a growth trajectory through a strong capital campaign, the re-emergence of child and youth programs, a stronger missions outreach program, and an overall re-invigorated spirit and approach. This would come through both the religious and lay leadership in the church. Four years after Jon raised the issue, some of the things he wanted to accomplish are now being done. He'd be happy to see former members returning and newcomers in the pews.

People do matter, and so do the numbers.

Thank you, Jon, for planting the seed.

Jane's Commentary

Peter is saying in this chapter that the process of growing your church has to be systematic and cannot depend on the old adage, "build it and they will come." In some populations where community growth is booming, maybe "build it and they will come" does meet success. Or at least, it sort of works. But in most of today's communities, churches compete with every other institution for committed members, or as a salesperson like Peter might say—we compete for customers. Therefore, a careful and organized approach to church growth is needed.

Peter describes a common reaction from the clergy. In his chapter, the pastor responds by saying she is "not in sales." I do, of course, disagree. A pastor is most definitely in sales. A pastor has many other roles as well—pastor, teacher, and counselor, for example. But, like it or not, you are also a salesperson. Isn't it better to embrace that role and give it all you've got, than to watch your church slowly slip away?

Making it Happen Worksheet

List three ways you are a salesperson

1. _____

2. _____

3. _____

Identify your best sales strength.

_____

_____

_____

Practice that one three times this week.

Chapter Twenty One
The Final 120 Seconds, According to Peter

By Peter

Sitting in the second-to-last pew at the back of the church during a recent service, I was struck by how far our church has come in six months and how much it has grown.

The pews were filled, the space bright and welcoming, and the sounds were rich and loud. Ann, a long-time member of the church tapped me on the shoulder and whispered "Can you believe how many people are here today? I love what Jane has done for our church!"

The multiple bottles of hand sanitizer that once adorned every windowsill under the stained glass windows at either side of the sanctuary were now gone. An *Everyone Welcome Here* tapestry signaled a warm greeting to those coming through the front doors. The choir had expanded so much that chairs had to be brought in to give the new recruits a place to sit. And the church calendar was filled nearly every night with meetings or gatherings of one kind or another: Trustees, Cabinet, Missions, Boy Scouts, Girl Scouts, Christian Ed, Pastoral Relations, Capital Projects Team, Annual Harvest Fair, Welcoming Committee … and the list goes on.

But our work of growing this church is far from done.

We still have a drafty gap at the top of one of the front doors that lets in frigid air on winter days. We have more exterior painting to do, and of course the beautiful antique clock at the back of the sanctuary still tells the right time only twice a day—the clock hands are more interested in napping than moving.

Almost two years ago we teetered on the brink of what seemed like an interminable search process. Yet, it wasn't too bad after all. We finished the job in fifteen months and found the right person: Reverend Jane.

The calling was followed by a successful negotiation process that resulted in a mutually acceptable agreement and contract. After the buzz of the so-called honeymoon period drifted away, we settled into her strong leadership, her style, grace, and conviction, her historical religious knowledge, and her caring for the here-and-now in everyone's lives. This approach is bearing fruit for the congregation.

The congregation is taking on a new personality, a new conviction to serve, a new deliberate method of welcoming and opening the doors to all. Now more than ever during the twenty-six years I've been a member of this church, it is a place of love, community, and fellowship; a place to seek calm, a place to gain reassurance and support, a place to learn, and a place to give.

No one person can grow and vitalize a church. Doing so takes a legion of volunteers and staff working in tandem to live out the Gospel. Yet, in my opinion, we do need the right kind of leader to mobilize and energize us and make things happen. That's exactly what Reverend Jane has been able to do.

A brief, powerful two minute event on one particular Sunday characterized it for me.

It started at 10:16 a.m.

At the conclusion of a moving anthem sung by our choir, Reverend Jane let the last triumphant note come to rest in the minds of the congregation. The silence was punctuated only by the tick-tock of that old clock at the back of the sanctuary. She then approached the pulpit and said quietly, "I don't think I even need to give a sermon after that. The choir's anthem may be all the sermon we need."

This was such a poignant moment. It wasn't about her; it was about the church, the music, the choir, the hymn, and the message from God met by our understanding and appreciation. So, while that moment of grace wasn't about her, it was reflective of her leadership style, her presence, and her influence.

At 10:18 a.m. as Reverend Jane introduced her sermon, she interjected a hilarious vignette that brought a loud wave of laughter from the congregation and filled the church with boisterous energy, in stark contrast to the quiet, deep introspection in the moments after the hymn.

Nearly crying one moment; laughing the next. We were absolutely engaged and listening!

That two minute interval was a microcosm of what Jane has brought to this church. She is emotional, empathetic, supportive, positive, strong, and hopeful. She is a true leader; the key component to church growth. As a new moderator takes over and other members continue the enduring tradition of lay leadership and commitment to the cause, the steady and consistent leadership of Reverend Jane will continue to grow this church toward everything it can be, and God wants it to be.

Chapter Twenty Two
The Final 120 Seconds, According to Jane

By Jane

At the time of writing this final chapter, I have been at the Grafton Congregational Church for six months. The beginning was a whirlwind of emotion: leaving my previous congregation, moving from the midwest to the east coast, settling into an 1840's parsonage with creaking floors and drafty rooms, and jumping headfirst into the activities of Advent with a new and expectant congregation.

Immediately, I began assessing the congregation for potential growth. When I first walked through the church building, I noticed a few red flags that might impede growth, especially the tired state of the church's physical structure. The building's physical exhaustion was in direct contrast to the energy of the church members. The worship service seemed intent on making announcements with a board-meeting-like atmosphere. This felt to me like a congregation standing at a crossroads—either taking off and growing or plunging further into decline. I felt as if the church could go either way with the smallest push. I began to push.

And it has been relatively easy. I changed almost everything about the worship service (to the anxiety and chagrin of many), cleaned and re-cleaned the building (some I did myself and other cleaning I organized with groups), formed a welcoming committee, put a few key people into new leadership positions, and did my best to bolster the efforts of those who worked so hard to keep the church alive and stable during the long pastoral search. I wanted to release the energy and joy I could feel pulsing just under the surface. Some of my changes caused true consternation and ended in criticism of me. Other changes were welcomed and embraced.

An early meeting of the governing board was especially difficult. Three members made it abundantly clear they did not like my changes. I tried to explain my reasons and stay objective. But I came away from the meeting feeling discouraged and questioning myself. However, that response—theirs and mine— goes with the territory. You can't grow your church without making change, and changing things can result (will result) in unhappy church members.

But six months have gone by and I think we're all adjusting to the changes. More and more people seem on board with everything. At this writing, twelve people have joined the church. If twelve people join every six months, the size of the congregation will double in five years.

Attracting a steady stream (or even a trickle) of new members calls for an awareness of the essential ingredients for church growth. Every week I ask myself:

- Are my sermons engaging?

- Is worship friendly and meaningful to all people?

- Are we doing follow-up and response to visitors?

- Are we incorporating new members into the life of the church or dropping them like hot potatoes once they join?

♦ Am I available to new people to talk and find out more about who we are?

♦ Am I guiding the congregation toward growth in everything I do?

Growing a church is an everyday event—worth every bit of energy you put into it.

Jump start your church!

About the Authors

Peter G. Dennis is the Moderator at the Congregational Church of Grafton, Massachusetts, United Church of Christ. He is also the President of PMD Sales Training & Consulting, Inc., a Westborough, Massachusetts-based firm he founded in 2008. The firm specializes in sales training and consulting services to companies through a broad range of industries. His 28-plus years of sales experience includes senior positions with Veritude, a Fidelity Investments company, and CDI Corporation, a Philadelphia-based staffing and consulting organization. He is the author of *The Golden 120 Seconds of Every Sales Call*, published by NorLightsPress.

Peter and his wife Mary live in Grafton, Massachusetts. They have two daughters Sophie and Hilary, and an Australian Shepherd named Reggie.

Reverend Jane Willan is Pastor of the Congregational Church of Grafton, Massachusetts, United Church of Christ. Her ten-year career as a minister began in a small town in rural Iowa where she grew a small and struggling church into a thriving congregation. Since then she has pastored two more churches, leading each into exciting revitalization—even when the odds were against growth.

Jane has served a variety of leadership positions, all of which helped her envision a vibrant future for her churches. As Moderator of the Iowa Conference Board of Directors, United Church of Christ, and a member of the Board of Directors for

Justice and Witness Ministries, a National Board for the United Church of Christ, she learned how good leadership can affect the growth of a church.

Jane has a Master's of Science degree from Boston University, and a Master's of Divinity from Vanderbilt Divinity School. She lives in a 130-year-old church parsonage with her husband Don and two dogs, Magi and Moses.

CPSIA information can be obtained at www.ICGtesting.com
Printed in the USA
LVOW08s1102091014

408047LV00011B/66/P

9 781935 254942